Interactive Writing
& Interactive Editing

Making Connections between Writing and Reading

Stanley L. Swartz, Adria F. Klein, & Rebecca E. Shook

With contributions by:

Marie Belt, Karen Bunnell, Charlene Huntley, Cinda Moon,
Jan Schall, & Debra Wakefield

Dominie Press, Inc.

Acknowledgments

The authors would like to thank the many CELL and ExLL teachers and Literacy Coordinators whose ideas contributed to the activities featured in this book. Our admiration for this group and their hard work is boundless. Foundation staff members Amie MacPherson, Cathleen Geraghty, and Laurie Roach provided critical support to this project, as they do for all our projects. Our thanks to them. Anita Gronewald was our able typist, and Janet Maule Swartz provided valuable suggestions and critical review.

Publisher: Raymond Yuen
Editor: Bob Rowland
Designer: Natalie Chupil

Photo Credits: Nick Baker

Published by:

 **Dominie Press, Inc.**

1949 Kellogg Avenue
Carlsbad, California 92008 USA

www.dominie.com

ISBN 0-7685-0534-8
Printed in Singapore by PH Productions Pte Ltd
1 2 3 4 5 6 PH 03 02 01

Table of Contents

About the Authors

Dr. Stanley L. Swartz is professor of education at California State University, San Bernardino, and Director of the Foundation for California Early Literacy Learning that sponsors the CELL, Extended Literacy Learning (ExLL), and Second Chance for Literacy Learning professional development programs. Dr. Swartz is the author of the *Marine Life for Young Readers* series, co-author of *Building Blocks of Beginning Literacy,* and the editor of the *Carousel Readers* and *Teacher's Choice* series, all published by Dominie Press.

Dr. Adria F. Klein is professor emeritus of reading education at California State University, San Bernardino. Dr. Klein is the Trainer and Coordinator of ExLL and Second Chance for the Foundation for California Early Literacy Learning. Dr. Klein is published by Dominie Press and is the co-editor of the *Factivity Series*, co-author of *Building Blocks of Beginning Literacy*, and a contributor to the *Carousel Readers*.

Rebecca E. Shook is the Coordinator and CELL Trainer for the Foundation for California Early Literacy Learning. She is a co-author of the Dominie Press *Building Blocks of Beginning Literacy* and a contributor to the *Carousel Readers*. She has been an elementary teacher and principal, a county office consultant, and a Reading Recovery™ Teacher Leader. She now divides her time between training activities and coaching teachers in their literacy efforts.

About the Contributing Authors

All of the contributing authors are trainers for the Foundation for California Early Literacy Learning.

Marie Belt is a reading intervention specialist for the Fontana, California School District. She has been a teacher in the primary grades for 17 years and a CELL Literacy Coordinator.

Karen Bunnell holds a master's degree in education and has more than 16 years of experience teaching in elementary classrooms. She has also worked as a mathematics consultant, mentor teacher, and staff developer.

Charlene Huntley has taught for 20 years in both special education and regular classrooms ranging from early primary to nontraditional adult classrooms. She is a teacher and CELL/ExLL Literacy Coordinator in Sheridan, Wyoming.

Cinda Moon has been a primary grades teacher for 18 years. She has also been a Reading Recovery™ teacher and a CELL Literacy Coordinator.

Jan Schall is the coordinator of literacy programs for the Yucaipa-Calimesa, California School District. She is also a Reading Recovery™ Teacher Leader.

Debra Wakefield has taught primary grades in Crescent City, California for the past 25 years. She is currently the CELL Literacy Coordinator for Joe Hamilton School in the Del Norte County School District.

Note to Teachers

Helping children learn to read and write is our most important responsibility as teachers. Reading and writing are the foundation on which all later learning is built. Through reading we are able to receive and understand the messages of others. Through writing we are able to send our own messages to someone else.

There are many ways to support children as they learn to read and write. From the development of oral language and understanding the phonology of the language to the ability to read and write complex text, teachers have various teaching methods available for their use.

The primary purpose of this text is to provide an introductory look at two exciting and powerful methods used to teach children to write: interactive writing and interactive editing. Unlike any other teaching methods that we know, interactive writing and interactive editing engage the teacher and the children in a collaborative process of learning the necessary skills to be a good writer, and by extension, a good reader. The value and power of these teaching methods are limited only by our ability to use them. We hope that this book can help increase your understanding and support your use of interactive writing and interactive editing.

The book is organized into three major sections. Sections one and two detail the procedures for interactive writing and interactive editing. Both of these sections include a definition and introduction to the teaching method, a step-by-step description of how to begin using the method, and a detailed description of procedures. In addition, a collection of sample lessons, including photographs, is included for both interactive writing and interactive editing. The Assessment section includes a Writing Checklist, Procedural Checklist, and a Writing Rubric. The appendices contain a Handwriting Model and Phonics Skill Charts.

in•ter•ac•tive wri•ting
\in-te-ˋrak-tiv rit-in\   *n.*
1: A teaching method in which children and teacher negotiate what they are going to write and then share the pen to construct the message. **2:** A powerful way to support literacy learning in children.

1. About Interactive Writing

What single teaching method can be used to support the development of phonological skills and help children attach meaning to print? How can teachers develop a lesson that allows whole group instruction and individual attention at the same time? How can the teacher practice skills without losing the excitement and enthusiasm of the class? How can we learn to read and write and still have fun? The answer to these questions is interactive writing.

Interactive writing is a cooperative event in which teacher and children jointly compose and write text. Not only do they share the decision about what they are going to write, they also share the duties of scribe. The teacher uses the interactive writing session to model reading and writing strategies as he or she engages children in creating text.

INTERACTIVE WRITING IS:

Negotiating the composition of texts

Collaborating in the construction of text

Using the conventions of print

Reading and rereading texts

Searching, checking, and confirming while reading and writing

Interactive writing can be used to demonstrate concepts about print, develop strategies, and learn how words work. It provides children with opportunities to hear sounds in words and connect those sounds with corresponding letters. Students are engaged in the encoding process of writing and the decoding process of reading, all within the same piece of text. Interactive writing is a unique opportunity to help children see the relationship between reading and writing.

USES OF INTERACTIVE WRITING

Direct and explicit instruction in phonology and word analysis

Teach children how written text works

Teach children the connections between what we write and read

During the interactive writing process, students and the teacher talk about what they are going to write. The teacher serves as the facilitator of the discussion—guiding, modeling, adding, summarizing, confirming, combining, and synthesizing the children's ideas. As the actual writing begins, many opportunities for specific teaching are available. The goal is to get the children's thoughts on paper, discussing the topic and the process of writing, dealing with the conventions of print, and working on grammar, spelling, punctuation, letter formation, phonics, and voice. As children become more proficient writers, lessons can focus on style and writing for different purposes.

The finished writing is displayed in a way that allows for continued use as a text for shared reading or independent reading. The work is not as neat as teacher writing or commercial posters, but children are more likely to use it as a source of information because of the

VALUES OF INTERACTIVE WRITING

Demonstrates concepts about print, early strategies, and how words work

Provides opportunities to hear sounds in words and connect sounds with letters

Helps children understand the decoding and encoding process in reading and writing

Increases spelling knowledge

ownership that comes with their involvement in the writing process. The goal of interactive writing is that the skills learned will transfer to students' independent writing and support the development of reading skills as well.

There is no one right way to do interactive writing. Interactive writing involves teacher choices based on observation of student needs, and uses the grade level curriculum and district and state standards. Teachers can begin with basic procedures and use interactive writing for more advanced purposes as they become more familiar with the procedures.

2. Getting Started

Step 1

Children are generally seated on the floor in front of the chart paper that will be used for writing.

Use a group activity to initiate the interactive writing process.

This might be reading a story aloud or having a discussion about a shared experience or classroom activity.

Step 2

Talk about points of interest in the story or activity. Encourage the children to share their experiences in relation to the story or express their opinions.

Remember that the oral language used during this discussion will be a rich source for the interactive writing piece.

Step 3

Tell the children that you would like them to write about their ideas related to the story or activity.

Discuss with the children what they might want to write.

Ask the children to give suggestions about what they are going to write.

Ask the children how they want to start their story.

Step 4

Develop consensus on the exact wording that will be used. This is called negotiation.

Note: There are several steps that will help with the negotiation process.
- *The actual wording of the text needs to come from the children.*
- *The teacher should lead the discussion and give input throughout the negotiation.*
- *Give an opportunity for all ideas to be heard.*
- *Remember that this should be a true negotiation, even though there might be a specific teaching point that the teacher wants to build into the activity.*

Step 5

Repeat the sentence and enunciate each word carefully.

To make sure that the children know the exact wording and language that has been negotiated, repeat the sentence two or three times. Have the children repeat the sentence with the teacher.

Step 6

Write down the exact wording that was negotiated.

This is not for the children, but for the teacher to use during the writing. Even though the teacher will repeat the negotiated sentence a number of times during the writing, it is helpful to have a written reminder.

After the negotiation process, begin the actual writing.

Note: During the writing the teacher and the children share the responsibility for the writing.

Step 7

When picking a child to write, pick one who will be successful.

Based on what the child can do, ask him or her to contribute a letter, a part of a word, a whole word, or even multiple words.

Note: Remember that there are two tasks during the writing. First, support the child who is writing to ensure success, and second, use this time as an opportunity to make various teaching points to the rest of the class.

Step 8

Use various methods to help the children think about words and how they are made.

Stretching Words

Ask the children to say a word slowly, stretching it so that they can hear the sounds.

Note: Some teachers slowly spread their hands to help children think about stretching words.

Analogy

Ask the class to try to spell a new word, using a word they already know. This is called analogy.

Note: Onset and rime are very useful to help children make an analogy and make new words from old words they know. Example: "If you can spell cook, then you can spell took or look." The use of a Magna Doodle, magnetic letters, or white board can be very useful for this work.

Step 9

Tell the children that some words are used so often that we need to memorize them and have them in our head. Use examples from the text that is being written.

Note: The high frequency words that the children are expected to know are written as whole words.

Of course all writers make mistakes, and interactive writing is certainly no exception. Use white correction tape for mistakes. When a child makes a mistake, just cover it up and make the correction, or allow the child to correct it.

Note: The finished interactive writing piece should not have spelling mistakes. The children will be using it as a model for both reading and writing, so it is essential that it is correct. Most corrections should be made at the point of error to help focus on the teaching point.

Step 10

Repeat steps 8 and 9 as the teacher and children continue to work on the text, deciding both which spelling strategy to use and what teaching points to make.

Note: The amount of text that is completed in one setting will vary, based on the group. One sentence might be all that is completed in one lesson. If this is the case just pick up where the text left off on subsequent lessons. On other days, two or three sentences, or even more, might be finished. Remember, it is better to stop the task before interest and enthusiasm decrease.

Step 11

Teaching Points

As the selected child writes on the chart, focus back to the group and make appropriate teaching points.

Encourage young children to air write (write letters in the air) or practice their letter formation on the floor.

Note: It is important to keep the group engaged during this step to ensure participation. Keep the discussion lively, and involve as many children as possible.

Step 12

Do mini lessons as an extension of Step 11.

The lessons can take many forms that extend learning (examples: word work, types of writing, language usage, sentence complexity, developing voice, and paragraph development).

Note: A Magna Doodle, white board, or magnetic letters can be very helpful. Make sure all the children in the group can see the work being demonstrated on the board.

Step 13

Direct the children's attention to other writing in the room that supports the teaching point that is being made.

This writing can be word walls, shared readings, previous interactive writings, or any large print you have displayed in the room that the children are familiar with.

Note: Using the resources of the room is the first step to independence. This helps children transition from using the teacher as a source to thinking of ways they can solve their own problem or answer their own question about letter formation, spelling, or word choice.

Step 14

Reread the work with the children after **each** addition to the text. Use a pointer to follow word by word.

Rereading provides an opportunity for appropriate language structure to guide the construction of text.

Note: Rereading is an important step and helps maintain the continuity of the writing. Children who are working on directionality and one-to-one matching will need to point and read word by word. A transition step as children become more proficient would be to point to the beginning of each line as it is read.

Step 15

Reread the text and model fluency.

Reread with the whole group for fluency, expression, comprehension, and continuity.

Note: Fluent reading might get lost in all of the word work. It is important to model and practice fluent reading.

Step 16

Display the completed writing.

Note: As the work is in progress it should remain on the easel, prominently displayed. The completed interactive writing should be attractively displayed. It needs to be easily accessible for children to reread and use as a resource for future writing.

Completed work can be displayed on the bulletin board with illustrations added by the children.

As more interactive writing is completed, earlier work can be taken down and made into a big book to use as a shared reading or for independent reading.

Smaller versions of the big book can be created so that the children can have individual copies.

3. Interactive Writing Procedures

Before the Writing

Classroom Setup

An area of the classroom should be designated for interactive writing. This area should have easy access to resources in the room. These resources include a name chart and an ABC chart for beginners and a word wall for both beginners and more proficient children. Every child should have an unobstructed view of the interactive writing chart and the teacher. Children need enough room to be able to come forward and write on the chart.

Seating arrangements vary according to individual teaching style and preference and the composition of the class. These can range from sitting on the floor to sitting on chairs in semicircle rows. Some teachers allow random student choice of where to sit and others maintain a seating plan. Special education teachers and reading specialists working in small groups might have children sit at a table.

Classroom Setup

Name chart
Student names arranged alphabetically in a pocket chart or on chart paper

ABC chart of both lower and upper case letters

Word wall
Display of high frequency and high utility words in an alphabetic list

Interactive writing
Display of other completed writing

Setting the Instructional Purpose

Interactive writing lessons should always have more than one instructional purpose. For beginning writers, emphasizing concepts about print and how to stretch words and hear the sounds will be a starting point. Other instructional purposes should be identified before the writing and contributed by the teacher in the discussion about what to write. The teaching points of the lesson are carefully chosen based on the needs of the children as determined by teacher observation during independent writing, independent reading, and guided reading.

Beginning Points for Interactive Writing

There are many ways to start an interactive writing. These are some ideas that might serve as beginning points:

- A story read to the children.
- Content area reading such as science, social studies, history, math, or health.
- In response to an activity such as cooking, art, a visitor, or field trip.
- To fill a classroom need such as alphabet charts, class rules, or informational chart.
- A nursery rhyme, poem, or song.
- Specific teaching points on conventions, contractions, homophones, topic sentences, paragraphs, or phonic elements.
- A class discussion on a current event or interest.

What Happens Before the Interactive Writing

A story is read aloud several times or a hands-on experience is used as the basis for writing.

There are extensive prewriting discussions to decide on what to write.

Types of Interactive Writing

Once the instructional purpose has been established there are three types of interactive writing to choose from: transcription, innovation, and negotiation. Each is more suited to particular types of writing.

Star light, star bright
First star I see tonight.
I wish I may, I wish I might,
Have this wish I wish tonight.

Transcription

In this type of interactive writing, text is taken from a poem, nursery rhyme, song, chant, or book. The task is to work together to write the exact wording of the original text. This is **not** a copying task. The interactive writing procedures should be used. Because the text is committed to memory, it is easier for the teacher to focus on specific teaching points and the writing process.

Transcription is a type of interactive writing that is particularly suited to very young children. Transcription avoids long discussions on what to write and helps maintain focus on the actual process and the word work involved.

Innovation

The task in this type of interactive writing is to change some part of a text that is familiar or has been read previously. The same structure, pattern, or language is used, but a different ending or twist might be added. Children are encouraged to be creative in using the existing format such as they might find in a poem.

Row, row, row your boat
Gently down the stream
becomes
Ride, ride, ride your bike
Safely down the street

Negotiation

In this type of interactive writing wholly new original text is created. The teacher and the children work together to develop a writing piece based on a shared book or experience. All aspects of the writing are negotiated: topic, genre, word choice, and word order.

In negotiation:

- The actual wording of the text comes from the children.
- The teacher leads the discussion and makes suggestions regarding grammar, extending vocabulary, and sentence complexity.
- The teacher gives the opportunity for all ideas to be heard.
- The teacher participates but makes sure that it is a true negotiation.

Three Types of Interactive Writing

Transcription	Reconstruct existing text
Innovation	Change a familiar text
Negotiation	Original composition

Choosing a Format

After the selection of interactive writing type has been made, discuss with the class what type of paper to use and what the future plans for the piece might be. Will it become a chart, big book, or wall hanging? Think about placement of the text. Will this placement work when the piece is cut to transform it from a bulletin board to a big book? Take a few moments to plan ahead, and lost time and inconvenience will be avoided.

The printing on the interactive writing needs to be large enough for all the children to see easily. Again, think about the future plans for the piece. If it is going to be up on the wall, the printing needs to be quite large. After these decisions have been made, the writing can begin.

Interactive Writing Materials

Required	Optional
Chart paper	Easel
Markers	Magna Doodle
Correction Tape	White Board or Chalk Board
Pointer	Magnetic Letters and Board

Materials for Interactive Writing

The only materials that are absolutely necessary for interactive writing are something to write with and something to write on. It is not uncommon for teachers to improvise or make do with what they have. Chart paper and markers are useful because they help the whole class see the work in progress. Correction tape is helpful for maintaining the flow of the writing by making a quick correction and rewrite at the point of error. A pointer helps you point to the text so that all the children can see. Many teachers like to use an easel to hold the chart paper; others simply tape the chart paper to the board or wall. Teaching aids like a Magna Doodle, other writing board, or magnetic letters are convenient and add variety to the ways teaching points can be made. However, the process is more important than the availability of any particular material.

During the Writing

In interactive writing the teacher and the students share the responsibility (and the pen) for the writing. It is important to remember that the interactive writing lesson is not focused on the child who is writing, but rather on the class. Choose a child who will be successful, based on assessments and observations. The interactive writing lesson is directed to the class as they observe the writer, talk about the piece in progress, and respond to teaching points. Model and discuss with the children what they are expected to do when they are writing on their own. Careful monitoring of independent writing will increase understanding of each individual student's strengths and weaknesses. For example, if one or more children do not use periods correctly in their independent writing, the next interactive writing is a good opportunity to make this a teaching point.

What Happens During the Interactive Writing

The children and teacher share the role as scribe.

The teacher models reading and writing strategies as children are engaged in creating text.

The goal of the writing is to develop children's independent reading and writing strategies.

This writing is used as a text for children to reread.

The finished text is generally a few sentences in length.

The writing of a single text occurs over several days.

The writing itself is a combination of children's writing and teacher's writing. This will mean an end product that is not as neat as teacher-produced writing or commercial print and posters. But the connections children make with something they actually wrote are an important consideration. The teacher is reminded to contribute to the writing throughout the process. Contributions should be made at all levels, including: when the children do not know the construction of a word; when a teacher contribution helps maintain flow; and possibly when all of the children can write the word.

Classroom Management

Interactive writing needs to be paced at an appropriate level to ensure that all students will remain engaged and thinking about the work in progress. Pacing needs to be quick throughout the lesson. Children can become restless while another child writes, so teaching time and text construction must be balanced. As a general rule, praising children for their ideas and contributions encourages participation to a greater

degree than reprimands. Positive attention and reinforcement to appropriate behaviors is more likely to yield the desired results than a negative focus on inappropriate behaviors.

Student talking during interactive writing is important, but the teacher plays the role of facilitator and needs to keep the discussion on track and meaningful. The establishment of routines that are familiar to everyone will allow for maximum interaction. Teacher preference and style vary, and so will the routines. Some teachers are more formal and ask students to raise their hands before contributing; other teachers are comfortable with a more informal style that allows children to speak out. Regardless of these variations the key is to establish a standard of behavior that allows students to interact while maintaining focus on the task.

Using the Room as a Resource

Making a classroom a literate environment means more than having books and other reading material readily available for children to use. It also means an environment where print displayed in the room becomes a source of information for children. Children should be asked to consider previous interactive writing that might have a word or spelling pattern that is under consideration in a writing in progress. Children are encouraged to think about things they have read and how that information can be used during writing. The word wall, charts, and other print displayed in the room take on a new importance in fostering independence in children. Problem solving that is not teacher centered is an important goal in interactive writing, with the expectation that this skill will transfer to independent writing.

Keeping Everyone Engaged During the Writing

- *Make sure the topic is one of interest.*
- *Allow for extensive conversation.*
- *Send children to find a letter or word in the room.*
- *Use the name chart, ABC chart, and word wall.*
- *Keep students active with air writing or writing on the carpet.*
- *Ask questions to keep children thinking about the writing.*
- *Show your own enjoyment and enthusiasm.*

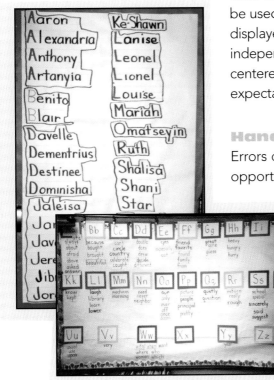

Handling Errors

Errors during interactive writing are important teaching opportunities. Though children who will be successful should be selected to write, errors will be inevitable. A roll of white correction tape is recommended to cover the error. Make the correction immediately at the point of error and treat it as a natural part of writing. If the teacher models this attitude, the children will do the same. It is important that the end product not contain errors. These pieces will be displayed and used as a resource, since correct models are important.

Teaching Points

Teaching points should be very direct and explicit. Use concrete examples that are in the context of the work in progress. Sometimes a discussion is the best way to make a teaching point, and often a demonstration works best.

These mini lessons conducted during interactive writing are the power of the process. Children are learning what they need to know to complete this task rather than skill learning that is isolated and disconnected from need. Concrete examples are usually best, and aids like a Magna Doodle, magnetic letters, and transparent highlight tape can help children focus on the instruction. This is also a good time to direct the attention of the children to other resources in the room. Word walls, shared readings, and previous interactive writings can serve as reminders to children about how the work in progress is connected to other work they have done.

Useful Prompts During Interactive Writing

- *If it's in your head, just write it.*
- *If it's not in your head, what should you try?*
- *Do you know where it is around the room? (Word wall, shared reading, interactive writings)*
- *Is it a word you can stretch and hear the sounds?*
- *Is it like a word you already know?*
- *Is it a combination word?*
- *Is there a part of the word you know and a part of the word you need to stretch?*
- *Can you break the word into syllables?*
- *Write one syllable at a time.*
- *Does it look right? (Prompt for after the word is written.)*

Alphabetic Principle

- *Letter recognition*
- *Letter formation (see Appendix A for Handwriting Model)*
- *Letter-name correspondence*
- *Letter-sound correspondence*
- *Alphabetic order*

Concepts About Print

- *Directionality*
- *One-to-one matching*
- *Return sweep*
- *Spacing*
- *Concept of first and last part of word, sentence, story*
- *Punctuation*

Alphabetic Principle

Beginning writers need to start at the beginning with letter recognition and letter formation. Children need to learn the names of letters and the sound that each letter makes. The order of letters in our alphabet is also important. Alphabet charts, name charts, and word walls are important resources for this learning.

Concepts About Print

Beginning writers also need to learn what print is and how it works. Remember that each of these concepts needs to be taught, and interactive writing is an effective way to accomplish the task.

Phonemic Awareness and Phonics

Interactive writing is an effective way to teach the important concepts of phonemic awareness and phonics. The phonology of the language is the starting point for beginning readers and writers. Students should say words slowly and listen for the sounds they hear in words (phonemic awareness). Instruction should be directed to associating these sounds with letters or groups of letters (phonics). As students engage in this process, you are modeling how to both build up (encode) and break down (decode) words.

Teaching decisions need to consider spelling and the best strategy for each word. Some words are phonetically regular and can be said slowly so that children can hear the sounds. Some words are phonetically irregular and need special attention. Many words can be best reached through knowledge of other words. High frequency words are ones that you expect children to memorize and write as a whole word (*I*, *a*, *and*, *said*, and *because* are examples).

Words that are phonetically regular can be stretched. Stretching words is a way to help children say words slowly and listen to the sounds. Teachers have different ways of helping children think of the term *stretching*. Some teachers have the children slowly stretch their hands apart as they say the word, while still others merely say the word slowly. Regardless of the method chosen, children need to have the idea of stretching a word and listening for sounds modeled. In interactive writing the teacher and the class stretch the word together. Some children may not hear all the sounds or may not hear the sounds in the proper sequence. In that case the teacher supplies the missing sounds or the correct sequence of sounds. After the first sound is written, the group stretches the word again and listens for the next sound. (Keep in mind that the sound they hear may be represented by a group of letters or spelling pattern such as *ing*, *sh*, *ch*, and *igh*.) Teachers need to be ready to supply those letters that some children are unable to hear.

It is important to help children think about using what they already know about some words to work on words that they do not know. Onset and rime is a way to help children think about what they really know about how words are spelled. For example, if you know how to spell *dog*, then you know how to spell *log* or *fog*. Interactive writing is a good opportunity to discuss spelling patterns, spelling irregularities, and word usage.

Written Language Conventions

Children will learn these conventions best as they participate in writing. Sentence structure, capitalization, and grammar are important concepts that become teaching points as the interactive writing proceeds and as the need arises in the text that is in progress.

Phonemic Awareness and Phonics

Hearing sounds in words

Inflectional endings

Rhyming

Syllabication

Compound words

Onset and rime

Segmentation

Chunking and blending

Root words

Sounds in sequence

Analogies

High frequency words

Spelling patterns

Consonants, blends, short and long vowels, digraphs, diphthongs

Alliteration

Suffixes, prefixes, root words

Writing Process

As children become more proficient, the writing process itself becomes the focus of attention. How do we develop an idea and get that idea in writing? How can aids like outlining or lists of key content words be used? The discussions with children go to much higher levels as they think about the many ways that their ideas can be expressed in their writing.

Finishing the Interactive Writing Piece

Written Language Skills

Punctuation and capitalization	Homophones, antonyms, synonyms
Spelling and word analysis	Parts of speech
Sentence structure	Word usage
Grammar	Irregular words
Similes and metaphors	Onomatopoeia
	Contractions

How much interactive writing is completed in one session is a teacher decision that is based on knowing the children in the group and what they are capable of completing in one sitting. It is not necessary to finish an interactive writing piece in one session. With young children the teacher might only negotiate one sentence, and with older children, two or three sentences or even a whole paragraph. One of the most important decisions to make is when to stop. When the children are no longer engaged, or the enthusiasm has waned, the interactive writing session should be ended. It is better to return to the work another day than to press beyond the point where children's attention and interest are lost.

Writing Process

Idea development	Concept development
Text organization	Characters, setting, plot
Proofreading and editing	Writing categories
Outlining	Paragraph development
Vocabulary and word choice	

Avoid thinking that the end product is the most important part of interactive writing. The opportunity to model what children need to learn and make direct teaching points is the focus of interactive writing. An interactive writing piece completed over several days or even a week is not unusual. The decision about how many sessions and the length of each session can change dramatically from group to group and even with the same group on different days.

In interactive writing, the process is as important as the product. It might be said that what we learn on the journey is more valuable than reaching the destination.

What Happens After the Interactive Writing

- *Writing is displayed and used for shared or independent reading.*

- *Children are encouraged to use the writing as a source of information.*

- *Strategies learned from interactive writing transfer to independent writing.*

- *The writing is used in extension activities such as story maps or class-made big books.*

After the Writing

Rereading Your Work

Interactive writing should be read and reread frequently while the piece is in progress and also when the piece is completed. Rereading can focus on early behaviors such as directionality and one-to-one matching as well as phrasing, comprehension, and fluency as children become more proficient. The rereading is an opportunity to model and support rather than a way to assess children's progress.

Uses for Completed Interactive Writing

Independent Writing

Use the interactive writing as the source or prompt for independent writing. Children should be encouraged to extend the interactive writing or write a new ending. Remind them to use what they have learned in interactive writing. Use of new learning should be transferred to independent writing. Children should be encouraged to refer to the interactive writing and use it as a source of information.

Shared Reading

Using interactive writing as a shared reading is an important way to make the connection between reading and writing. Teaching points that were made during the writing can be repeated, and ideas that did not come up can be made a part of the shared reading.

New and Review During Shared Reading

Teach concepts about print	*Word usage (to, too, two, there, their, they're)*
Work with word families	*Contractions*
Talk about a phonics rule	*Parts of speech*
Discuss word meaning	*Topic and supporting sentences*
Work on comprehension	*Phrasing*
Punctuation	*Fluency*
	Root words, prefixes, suffixes, metaphors, similes

Big Books

At some point there will be more interactive writing than available wall space or display opportunities. Without much work an interactive writing can be converted into a big book. Big books are an important resource for independent reading. The piece might be cut into pages and stapled. This also helps reinforce the connection between reading and writing. Children enjoy the opportunity to reread something that they helped write.

Individual Books

In addition to making big books, individual books can be created. Interactive writing can be cut to individual book size or in some cases reduced on a copy machine or even retyped on a computer. As with the creation of big books, children are interested in the book-making process and the connection between something they wrote and something they read.

Interactive Writing

Uses children's oral language to negotiate the composition of text.

Creates text based on common experiences.

Helps children see the connection between what we read and what we write.

Provides an opportunity to learn important skills in authentic ways.

Students in this class read the short vowel books from the Dominie series, *Building Blocks of Beginning Literacy: Sam's Cap, Ted's Letter, Bill's Trip, Fox's Box,* and *Lumpy Rug.* The interactive writing was generated as a result of reading the books and helping children use their ideas for both text and illustration.

4. Interactive Writing Activities

Activity 1
Alphabetic Principle
Letter Recognition

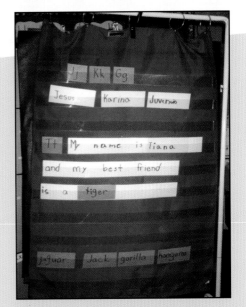

Students manipulate and read these sentences about themselves during literacy centers.

Goal
Students will recognize and name each letter of the alphabet.

Area of Study
Language Arts

Interactive Writing Type
Innovation

Resources
Variety of alphabet books, sentence strips
Pocket chart, name chart

Lessons

- Read aloud an alphabet book. Choose a book that has a repetitive pattern and displays capital and lowercase letters in enlarged text on each page.

- Determine that the class will create a literacy center, using the names of the students in the class.

- Establish a sentence pattern similar to the one in the book. Interactively write the sentence pattern on sentence strips and display them in a pocket chart.

- Direct the students to write their names on individual sentence strips. Collect the strips.

- Choose one student's name card. Ask the students to name the first letter of that student's name.

- Help the students to choose an animal name that begins with the same letter to complete the student's sentence. Use a lowercase letter as the first letter of that word.

- Write a matching capital and lowercase letter for each child's sentence. Read each sentence as it is completed. For example, "Tt, My name is Tiana, and my best friend is a tiger."

- Complete this activity over several days. Model the procedures of the center for the students. Remind them that the letter displayed must match the student's name and the animal displayed.

- Reread different sentences often, emphasizing letter names.

Extensions

- Have the students illustrate their own sentences. Use the sentences and illustrations to make a class book.

- Make name cards on sentence strips for each child. Take attendance in the morning by showing each child's name and saying, "Good morning, Rebecca. Rebecca starts with R."

Additional Resources
Bayer, J. *A My Name is Alice.* Penguin Putnam Books for Young Readers, 1984. ISBN 0803701233

Carlson, J. *ABC, I like Me.* Viking Penguin, 1997. ISBN 0670874582

Slate, J. *Miss Bindergarten Gets Ready for Kindergarten.* NAL, 1996. ISBN 0525454462

Activity 2
Alphabetic Principle
Letter Formation

Goal
Students will learn to form letters correctly and fluently.

Area of Study
Language Arts

Interactive Writing Type
Negotiation

Resources
A version of *Goldilocks and the Three Bears*
Painting materials

Lessons

- Read aloud a version of *Goldilocks and the Three Bears*.

- Determine that the class will create a class mural depicting scenes from the story.

- Determine which items and characters need to be painted, and list these interactively. These can be painted during literacy centers.

- Negotiate the text that will accompany the mural.

- As different letters are written throughout the lesson, demonstrate proper letter formation on a Magna Doodle. Use specific language to describe the letter strokes.

- Encourage the students to "write" letters that have been modeled. These can be written in the air, on the rug, on their friend's back. As students write, again verbalize specific directions for writing each letter correctly.

Extensions

- Encourage the students to use proper letter formation when writing independently.

- Provide different media for the students to use in the writing center to encourage writing (for example, chalkboard, white boards, markers, crayons, and colored pencils).

Additional Resources

Brett, J. *Goldilocks and the Three Bears*. Penguin Putnam Books for Young Readers, 1996. ISBN 0698113586

Ernst, L. *Goldilocks Returns*. Simon & Schuster Books for Young Children, 2000. ISBN 0689825374

Marshall, J. *Goldilocks and the Three Bears*. Penguin Putnam Inc., 1988. ISBN 0803705425

Students wrote their own version of *Goldilocks and the Three Bears*.

Activity 3
Alphabetic Principle
Letter-name Correspondence

Goal
Students will be able to name each letter of the alphabet.

Area of Study
Language Arts

Interactive Writing Type
Transcription

Resources
Various alphabet books to read aloud
Pictures to correspond with each letter of the alphabet
Name chart

Lessons
- Read aloud many alphabet books to the students and encourage conversation about letter names.

- Read the class name chart. Ask the students to point out and name any letter in their names that they know.

- Name and write each letter of the alphabet one at a time as a key picture is displayed.

- Direct the students to look at the class name chart as each new letter is written to discover who has that particular letter in their names. This lesson will take several days.

- Decide as a group how to arrange and display the letters in the classroom.

Extensions
- Make individual alphabet books, using the same pictures from the interactive writing for reinforcement of reading letter names independently.

- Make individual ABC charts for each child to take home, using a small version of the same pictures used in the interactive writing.

- Create a literacy center that allows students to search for and name the letters of the alphabet. Use colorful fly swatters and cut letter-sized holes in each. Encourage the students to search the text on display in the room for specific letters. Students work in pairs to catch the letters and name them.

Additional Resources
Kirk, D. *Miss Spider's ABC*. Scholastic, Inc., 1998. ISBN 0590282794

Martin, B., and Archambault, J. *Chicka Chicka Boom Boom*. Simon & Schuster, 1989. ISBN 067167949X

Most, B. *ABC T-Rex*. Harcourt, 2000. ISBN 0152020071

Walton, R. *So Many Bunnies: A Bedtime ABC and Counting Book*. Lothrop, Lee & Shepard Books, 1998. ISBN 0688136575

This example shows the lowercase alphabet written interactively in a kindergarten classroom. The alphabet is posted at eye level for students to see and refer to throughout the year.

Activity 4
Alphabetic Principle
Letter-sound Correspondence

Goal
Students will associate letters with their corresponding sounds.

Area of Study
Language Arts

Interactive Writing Type
Innovation

Resources
Variety of alphabet books

Lessons
- Read aloud a variety of alphabet books, particularly those that have many words beginning with the same letter.

- Point out and discuss the patterns in the books, particularly the use of names and first letter sounds.

- Establish a pattern by playing a name game such as, "B–my name is Bob and I like berries, balls, and boats."

- Determine that the class will write a book, following a pattern similar to the one in the book and using the names of the students in the class. Assist the students in establishing a pattern for their interactively written book.

- Write a page for each student in the class. Assist the students in using words that begin with the same letter as the person named.

- Discuss any variations in letter sounds as they come up naturally in discussions (for example, *giraffe* and *gorilla* begin with the letter *g*, but they represent different sounds).

Extensions
- Establish individual class alphabet books. Students can add pictures of their classmates to the appropriate page of their books. Later, they can add pictures of things that begin with the same sound.

- Direct the students to various activities with a prompt similar to, "Students whose names begin like *lollipop* can go out to recess."

These interactive writing pieces were first displayed in the room, and then reformatted into a class big book.

Additional Resources
Bennett, G., and Bennett, A. *The Best Alphabet Book in the West.* Arizona Highway Books, 1999. ISBN 0916179966

Ehlert, L. *Eating the Alphabet: Fruits and Vegetables From A to Z.* Harcourt, 1994. ISBN 0152009027

Hobbie, H. *Toot & Puddle (Puddle's ABC).* Little, Brown, and Company, 2000. ISBN 0316365939

Activity 5
Alphabetic Principle
Alphabetic Order

Goal

Students will be able to put the letters of the alphabet in sequential order.

Area of Study

Language Arts

Interactive Writing Type

Transcription

Resources

Alphabet books
Large paper holiday tree shape
Precut circles

Students' desire to make an ABC tree prompted this project.

Lessons

- Read aloud alphabet books with a holiday theme.

- Determine that the class will create a holiday tree to decorate the room. Each of the ornaments will display a letter of the alphabet.

- Name and write each letter in sequential order, one upper and matching lowercase letter on each precut circle.

- Decorate the letter ornaments and arrange them sequentially in alphabetical order on the tree.

Extensions

- Sing alphabet songs and chants that reinforce alphabetic order.

- Read additional alphabet books and perform an alphabet play.

- Create individual alphabet books to put into book boxes for independent reading or to take home.

- Create a literacy center that allows students to practice alphabetical order. Use holiday shapes, such as trees or ornaments, and write letters on each shape. Students can then arrange these shapes in alphabetical order.

Additional Resources

Bullard, L. *Not Enough Beds! (A Christmas Alphabet Book)*. Lerner Publishing Group, 1999. ISBN 157505356X

Hague, K. *Alphabears: An ABC Book*. Henry Holt & Company, Inc., 1991. ISBN 0805016376

Lionni, Leo. *The Alphabet Tree*. Alfred A. Knopf, 1990. ISBN 0679808353

Steer, D., Steer D., and Hawke, R. *Super Snappy ABC*. Millbrook Press, 2000. ISBN 076131430X

Activity 6
Concepts about Print
Directionality

Goal
Students will write and read text beginning from the left side.

Area of Study
Language Arts

Interactive Writing Type
Negotiation

Resources
Variety of books about Valentine's Day
Examples of valentines and messages

Lessons
- Read aloud various Valentine's Day books.

- Show actual valentines and read the messages.

- Decide that the students will write their own Valentine's Day message. Negotiate the message together.

- As each new word is added to the text, talk about where it should be placed on the paper.

- Reread the text frequently throughout the writing. Each time, prompt the students with questions such as, "Where do we begin reading?" and "Where do we go next?"

Extensions
- Provide materials for the students to make their own valentines and write personal messages.

Additional Resources
Carter, D. *Love Bugs*. Simon & Schuster Trade, 1994. ISBN 067186629X

London, J. *Froggy's First Kiss*. Penguin Putnam Books For Young Readers, 1999.   ISBN 0140565701

Roberts, B. *Valentine Mice*. Houghton Mifflin Company, 1997. ISBN 0395775183

Ross, D. *A Book of Kisses*. HarperCollins Children's Books, 1999. ISBN 0060281693

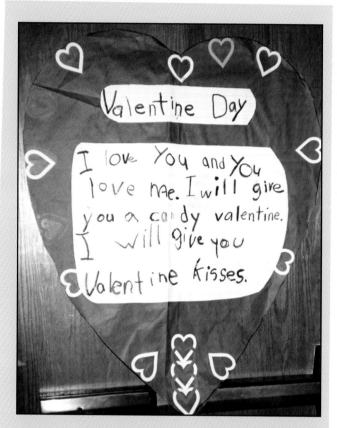

This example is posted near a literacy center where children can revisit it to write their own valentine messages. Even after Valentine's Day, it continues to be a useful piece to refer to for directionality in both reading and writing.

Activity 7
Concepts about Print
One-to-one Matching

Goal
Students will point to each word as it is read orally.

Areas of Study
Language Arts, Social Studies

Interactive Writing Type
Negotiation

Resources
Variety of books about farms
Enlarged picture of a farmer

Lessons
- Read aloud many books about farms.

- Ask the students to share what they know about farmers.

- Talk about how farmers look and how their clothes and tools are different than other community helpers.

- Using an enlarged shape of a farmer, negotiate labels for the farmer's clothes. Make sure the labels include adjectives so that the text is composed of short phrases rather than single words.

- As each new label is negotiated, make sure to count each word so that the students are made of aware of word boundaries.

- Reread the text with the students frequently, demonstrating how to point to each word as it is read.

- Encourage the children to practice one-to-one matching by asking individuals to point and lead the class in reading.

Extensions
- Create a literacy center that allows students to practice one-to-one matching skills. Provide a variety of pointers that they can use to "Read the Room," pointing to words as they read.

- Encourage the students to write additional text about farms and farmers.

Additional Resources
Brown, M.W. *Big Red Barn*. HarperCollins Children's Books, 1989. ISBN 0060207485

Ember, K., and Kleinberg, N. *Old MacDonald Had A Farm*. Western Publishing Company, Inc., 1997. ISBN 0307988066

Sloat, T. *Farmer Brown Goes Round and Round*. Darling Kindersley Publishing, Inc., 1999. ISBN 0789425122

Tafuri, N. *This Is The Farmer*. Greenwillow Books, 1994. ISBN 0688094686

Waddell, M. *Farmer Duck*. Candlewick Press, 1996. ISBN 1564025969

Children often return to their own writing to read while pointing carefully to each word.

Activity 8
Concepts about Print
Return Sweep

Goal
Students will read to the end of a line of text, and start at the beginning of the next line of text.

Areas of Study
Language Arts, Social Studies

Interactive Writing Type
Negotiation

Resources
Books with behavior themes

Lessons
- Have a class discussion about appropriate school behavior that would encourage friendship and learning.

- Read books that deal with behavior issues to enrich the conversation.

- Determine that the students will write a set of class rules.

- Determine these rules together, using language the students will understand. Negotiate text that will extend for more than one line of text.

- Write the rules interactively. As each sentence is written, discuss the proper place to begin writing. At the end of each line of text, discuss the need to return to the left side of the page to continue the writing process.

- Reread the text often. Talk again about what to do when students read to the end of a line of text.

Extensions
- Discuss return sweep again during many shared reading lessons.

- Provide ample opportunities for students to read texts during independent reading and literacy centers.

Additional Resources
Cuneo, D. *Mary Louise Loses Her Manners*. Random House Children's Books, 1999. ISBN 0440414458

Wells, R. *Timothy Goes to School*. Penguin Putnam Books for Young Readers, 1981. ISBN 0803789483

Zolotow, C. *My Friend John*. Random House Children's Books, 2000. ISBN 0385326513

These rules written during the first weeks of school were read and referred to often throughout the year.

Activity 9
Concepts about Print
Spacing

Goal
Students will write, using appropriate spacing between words.

Area of Study
Language Arts

Interactive Writing Type
Negotiation

Resources
A variety of cumulative stories

Lessons
- Read aloud several cumulative stories. Discuss each story and how it builds on itself.

- Suggest that the class could write their own cumulative story, based on one of the books that the students enjoyed.

- As each sentence is negotiated, repeat that sentence slowly several times, emphasizing each word.

- Write each sentence, emphasizing the concept of "wordness" while working through each word. The concept of "wordness" refers to appropriate use of spaces and the purpose for the spaces between words. Each space defines the word boundaries and tells the reader that the preceding word is complete.

- As each sentence is completed, have the students cut the words of the sentence apart. Again discuss the purpose of spaces in written text.

- Rebuild the text, leaving obvious spaces between the words.

Extensions
- Encourage the students to use spaces between words in their independent writing.

- Provide individual copies of the interactive writing text for each student. Ask the students to circle each word in the text.

Additional Resources
Downey, L. *The Flea's Sneeze*. Henry Holt and Company, 2000. ISBN 0805061037

Grossman, B. *My Little Sister Ate One Hare*. Crown Publishers, 1996. ISBN 0517596008

Hoberman, M. *The Eensy-Weensy Spider*. Little, Brown and Company, 2000. ISBN 0316363308

Wood, A. *The Napping House*. Harcourt Brace & Company, 1984. ISBN 01525670089

Spaces between words are clearly evident in this interactive writing piece.

Activity 12
concepts about Print
First and Last Part of a Story

Goal
Students will identify the first and last part of a story.

Area of Study
Language Arts

Interactive Writing Type
Negotiation

Resources
Favorite books

Lessons

- Read aloud a high-interest book.

- Encourage the students to share their favorite parts of the story and determine that the class will write about the students' favorite parts of the story.

- Once the students have determined their favorite parts, ask them to think about the order in which those events occurred in the story.

- Write the sentences interactively, in correct sequence. Stress the vocabulary *first, next,* and *last* in the discussion.

- Reread the text once it has been completed. Ask the students to point out the first and last part of the story.

Extensions

- Encourage the students to write their own summary of this story or another story. Remind them to include sentences that explain what happened first, next, and last in the story.

- Read aloud other books. Ask the students to identify the first and last parts of those stories.

Additional Resources

London, J. *Froggy Gets Dressed.* Puffin, 1995. ISBN 0140544577

Brumbeau, J. *The Quiltmaker's Gift.* Palace Press, Inc., 2000. ISBN 1570251991

Stevens, J. *Tops and Bottoms.* Harcourt Brace & Company, 1995. ISBN 0152928510

Froggy is a favorite character and a frequent topic for interactive writing with the children.

Activity 13
Concepts about Print
Punctuation

Goal
Students will identify different punctuation marks and their functions.

Areas of Study
Language Arts, Social Studies

Interactive Writing Type
Innovation

Resources
Variety of farm books

Lessons
- Read aloud a farm book with special attention to the punctuation.

- Invite the students to join in the reading.

- Encourage the students to write their ideas about the farm.

- Discuss the different punctuation marks needed to construct the text. Name the punctuation marks and their functions.

- Reread the text. Again locate the different punctuation marks and explain their functions. Reread fluently, using the punctuation.

- Illustrate the animals interactively written about during literacy centers.

Extensions
- Encourage the students to use different punctuation marks in their independent writing. Ask them to reread their writing fluently, using the punctuation to help them.

- Read other texts with similar punctuation during shared reading. Highlight the different punctuation marks with different colors of highlighter tape.

Additional Resources
Andrea, G. *Cock-a-doodle doo! Barnyard Hullabaloo.* Orchard Books, 1999. ISBN 1888444754

McDonnell, F. *I Love Animals.* Candlewick Press, 1996. ISBN 1564026620

Ziefert H. *Oh, What a Noisy Farm!* William Morrow & Company, 1995. ISBN 068813260X

This picture shows animal stories inspired by reading many farm books.

Activity 14
Concepts about Print
Punctuation

Goal
Students will identify different punctuation marks and explain their functions.

Area of Study
Language Arts

Interactive Writing Type
Negotiation

Resources
Completed interactive writing pieces
Shared reading texts

Lessons
- Reread a familiar shared reading or interactive writing text.

- Locate and highlight different punctuation marks used in the text. Remind the students of the function of the various punctuation marks.

- Determine with the students that the class will write a description of the different punctuation marks and their functions. These will then be used as resources for the students during interactive writing and independent writing.

- Negotiate sentences with the students that name each punctuation mark, and describe each punctuation mark's function. Remember to use the children's language when the sentences are written.

- Post the sentences, along with an enlarged version of each punctuation mark.

- Refer to these sentences frequently during interactive writing to encourage the students' understanding and independent use of the various punctuation marks.

Extensions
- Encourage the students to use appropriate punctuation in their independent writing. Prompt them to use this interactive writing as a resource.

- Continue to add different punctuation marks, as they are encountered in print.

Additional Resource
Dakos, K. *If You're Not Here, Please Raise Your Hand.* Aladdin Books, 1995. ISBN 0689801165

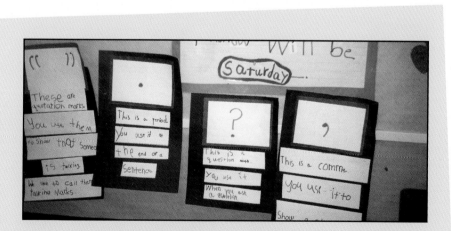

This interactive writing was referred to often during interactive writing and independent writing for use of punctuation marks.

Activity 15
Phonemic Awareness & Phonics
Hearing Sounds in Words

Goal
Students will stretch out words and listen for sounds they hear.

Areas of Study
Language Arts, Social Studies

Interactive Writing Type
Negotiation

Resources
Various poems and books about Thanksgiving
Large turkey shape
Paint

Lessons
- Read a variety of books to build background knowledge about Thanksgiving and the concept of being thankful.

- During discussion, prompt the students to think about things they are thankful for and happy about in their own lives.

- Encourage the students to think of a turkey that has bright colored feathers that they could personalize with their own ideas.

- As the negotiation progresses and ideas are decided upon, repeat each word to be written and carefully stretch out the word with the students so they are able to articulate the sounds they hear. Be sure that all the students articulate and stretch each word with the teacher. In the beginning, concentrate on the first sound of the word. Initial sounds can then be connected to children's names or other words they are familiar with.

- One or two words can be added to the turkey feathers each day.

- As new words are added, reread previously written words and ask the students to listen and name the beginning sound they hear.

Extensions
- Students can be encouraged to make their own book on the things they are happy and thankful for in a literacy center, using the class-made turkey as a resource.

- The interactive writing items from the turkey can be reproduced and put on cards. A corresponding picture of each item is put on another card. During literacy center time, students match the word with the picture.

This picture shows the painted turkey with all the things these kindergartners are happy for written on the feathers.

Additional Resources
Bauer, C.F. *Thanksgiving: Stories and Poems.* HarperCollins Publishers, Inc., 1994. ISBN 0060233265

Jackson, A. *I Know An Old Lady Who Swallowed A Pie.* Dutton Children's Books, 1997. ISBN 0525456457

Ropp, P., and Ropp, C. *Let's Celebrate Thanksgiving.* Millbrook Press, 1999. ISBN 0761304290

Rosen, M. *A Thanksgiving Wish.* Scholastic, Inc., 1999. ISBN 059025560

Activity 16
Phonemic Awareness & Phonics
Inflectional Endings

Goal
Students will add inflectional endings to root words.

Area of Study
Language Arts

Interactive Writing Type
Innovation

Resources
Predictable storybook with repetitive phrases
Magna Doodle

Lessons
- Choose a predictable book that contains repetitive phrases. The book should also contain examples of words that have inflectional endings, and it should be one that is enjoyable for the children to revisit often.

- After the students become familiar with the story, engage them in an interactive writing of an innovation of the text.

- During the negotiation, decide upon characters and story setting. Then focus discussion on the timing of the story. "Will we be writing it as if it is happening now (using the -ing ending) or as if it has already happened (using the -ed ending)?"

- Through this discussion, explain to the students that verb endings help us to know when an event took place, and that it is important to use similar verb endings throughout a piece.

- As the piece is negotiated and written, draw the students' attention to the verbs and prompt them to use appropriate verb tenses.

- When writing the verbs, use the Magna Doodle to demonstrate how to add inflectional endings to root words in order to get new words. Use known words, such as *play* to *played,* to demonstrate.

Extensions
- Paint characters and scenery to accompany the story. Display them on a bulletin board.

- Dramatize the interactive writing by making headbands of the characters and rereading the text.

- Create a literacy center that focuses on inflectional endings. Students read words from the word wall and search for verbs. Then they write the verbs and inflectional endings to create new words.

Additional Resources
Christelow, E. *Five Little Monkeys Jumping on the Bed.* Ticknor & Fields, 1991. ISBN 0899197698

Galdone, P. *The Gingerbread Boy.* Houghton Mifflin Company, 1979. ISBN 0395287995

Martin, B. *Brown Bear, Brown Bear, What Do You See?* Henry Holt & Company, 1983. ISBN 0805017445

Williams, S. *I Went Walking.* Harcourt, 1996. ISBN 0152007717

Students learned to add the inflections of *–ing* and *–ed* to verbs to create new words.

Activity 17
Phonemic Awareness & Phonics
Rhyming

Goal
Students will hear and identify rhyming words.

Areas of Study
Language Arts, Nursery Rhymes

Interactive Writing Type
Transcription

Resources
Various nursery rhyme books
Large shape of nursery rhyme character
Magna Doodle

Lessons

- Read aloud many nursery rhymes. Encourage the students to join in, singing and chanting rhymes.

- Reread the same rhymes many times, until the students become familiar with the nursery rhymes. On subsequent readings, pause at the rhyming words to see if the students begin to supply missing words.

- As the students are able to recite each of the nursery rhymes, engage them in an interactive writing of the rhymes.

- Discuss the idea that we can write and read things that we think and say.

- Talk about why the piece is called a rhyme, and point out the words that rhyme.

- When writing the rhyming words, elicit other rhyming words from the students.

- Write these additional rhyming words on the Magna Doodle, or have the students hear and recognize the rhyme at an aural level.

Extensions

- Reduce the actual interactive writing piece on a copy machine. Make copies that the students can keep in individual poetry books. Illustrate and read rhymes during independent reading time.

- Create literacy centers that focus on the nursery rhymes. Students can recite the rhymes while manipulating flannel board pieces, or they can create puppets to use for role-playing.

This nursery rhyme was sung, chanted, and read aloud many times before the actual interactive writing lesson took place.

- Create and paint nursery rhyme characters to add to the interactive writing display.

Additional Resources
Opie, I. *My Mother Goose Library*. Candlewick Press, 2000. ISBN 076361178

Trapani, I. *The Itsy Bitsy Spider*. Charlesbridge Publishing, Inc., 1992. ISBN 1879085771

Trelease, J., and Prelutsky, J. *Read Aloud Rhymes For the Very Young*. Alfred A. Knopf, 1986. ISBN 0394872185

Wright, B. F. *The Real Mother Goose*. Scholastic, Inc., 1994. ISBN 0590225170

Activity 18
Phonemic Awareness & Phonics
Syllabication

Goal
Students will say words aloud and clap their hands once for each syllable in each word.

Areas of Study
Language Arts, Science

Interactive Writing Type
Negotiation

Resources
Variety of books about weather

Lessons

- Read aloud many books about weather to introduce this unit of study.

- Encourage the students to recall words that describe different kinds of weather. Interactively write this list of words.

- As words are added to the list, draw the students' attention to the number of syllables in each word.

- Show the students how to break words into syllables by saying a word and clapping, one clap for each syllable. Demonstrate and then invite them to clap the words with you.

- Talk with the students about using this strategy to break multisyllabic words into manageable units when writing. They can then work with these smaller units and decide on an appropriate spelling strategy for each word chunk. Spelling of unknown words will become more accurate.

- Continue to add words to this list as a unit of study on weather takes place over several weeks. This list will then serve as a word bank for students to use during future interactive writing or independent writing.

Extensions

- Create a literacy center that allows students to practice pronouncing words and clapping syllables. Pictures, names of students in the class, or high frequency words can be made available for students to pronounce, clap, and then sort by number of syllables.

This is a first grade example of a list of words generated by students learning about the weather. The teacher demonstrated how to break long words into smaller parts.

- Encourage the students to write about the weather, using these words as a resource. As they write, prompt them to clap multisyllabic words and then work out the words, using the smaller word parts.

Additional Resources

Cech, J. *First Snow, Magic Snow.* Simon & Schuster Children's, 1992. ISBN 0027179710

Ellyard, D. *Weather* (The Nature Company Discoveries Library). Weldon Own Pty. Limited, 1996. ISBN 0809493705

Gibbons, G. *Weather Words and What They Mean.* Holiday House, Inc., 1996. ISBN 082340952X

Activity 19
Phonemic Awareness & Phonics
Compound Words

Goal
Students will identify compound words.

Areas of Study
Language Arts, Science

Interactive Writing Type
Negotiation

Resources
Variety of books about weather
Magna Doodle

Lessons

• As part of a unit of study on the weather, read aloud a variety of weather books. Engage the students in a discussion about the topic to build background knowledge.

• When the students have developed an understanding of weather concepts, engage them in an expository interactive writing piece on the topic.

• During the negotiation, ensure that several compound words are included in the text.

• As the text is written, focus on the compound words. As each compound word is added to the text, use the Magna Doodle to show how two smaller words can be combined to create a new and different word. As the students become familiar with the concept, ask them to generate examples of other compound words. Write these on the Magna Doodle and ask the students to point out the smaller words used to create the new word.

• Once the writing is completed, use the piece as a shared reading text. Locate the compound words and highlight them with highlighter tape. Two colors of tape may be used to clearly show each small word that makes up the new compound word.

Extensions

• Have a compound word search in which the students look for compound words in other texts around the room.

• Create a literacy center that focuses on compound words. Write words that can be put together to form compound words on sentence strips or colorful cutouts. Students manipulate pieces to form compound words and record them on a sheet of paper.

After the interactive writing, students used highlighter tape to identify the compound words in the text.

• Independently write a story that uses compound words.

• Negotiate a class definition for a compound word and write it interactively. Post the definition in the room and refer to it during interactive and independent writing.

• Engage the students in a compound word search. They may work in teams or independently to search any available text for compound words, which then may be recorded and shared with the class. Use these words to create a bank of compound words to be used as a resource.

Additional Resources

Ganeri, A. *The Usbourne Book of Weather Facts: Records, Lists, Facts, Comparisons.* EDCP, 1990. ISBN 086020975X

Martin, J.B. *Snowflake Bentley.* Houghton Mifflin Company, 1998. ISBN 0395861624

Upgren, A., Upgren, A., and Stock, J. *Weather: How It Works and Why It Matters.* Perseus Publishing, 2000. ISBN 0738202940

Williams, J. *The Weather Book.* Random House, Inc., 1997. ISBN 0679776656

Activity 20
Phonemic Awareness & Phonics
Onset and Rime

Goal
Students will use onset and rime to create new words.

Area of Study
Language Arts

Interactive Writing Type
Negotiation

Resources
Books about cookies
Highlighter tape
Magnetic letters

Lessons

- Read aloud books about cookies, keeping in mind the fact that -ook is a common rime that can be used to read and write many other words.

- Draw the students' attention to the -ook rime in the word *cookie*. Ask the students to brainstorm a list of words containing this rime. Interactively write the list of words.

- During the writing of the list, demonstrate the concept of onset and rime on the Magna Doodle or with magnetic letters. Explain that -ook is a chunk that occurs in other words. Knowing the word *cookie* can help students read and write more words that contain the -ook rime.

- Negotiate and interactively write silly stories using -ook words.

- Use the interactive writing as a shared reading, once it has been completed. The students will locate and highlight words that contain the -ook rime.

- Challenge the students to think of other words that work the same way. This lesson may be repeated with additional rimes until the students understand the concept.

Extensions

- Use student artwork to decorate the interactive piece with picture clues.

- Make additional lists of words that focus on a common rime.

- Make additional lists of words that use a common rime and interactively write silly stories with common rimes.

- Encourage the students to write other silly stories independently.

Here are four examples of onset and rime lists created by students in a first grade class. A picture cue that illustrates one of these high utility words is provided as additional support for emergent readers.

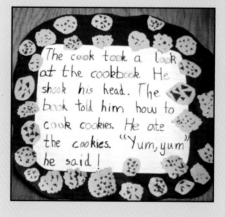

This big cookie looks good enough to eat but actually contains a silly story using –ook words.

Additional Resources

Bott, A. *A Cookie For the President*. Greene Bark Press, 1996. ISBN 1889851202

Lass, B. *Who Took the Cookies From the Cookie Jar?* Little, Brown & Company, 2000. ISBN 0316820164

Munsch, R. *MMM, Cookies!* Scholastic, Inc., 2000. ISBN 0590896032

Numeroff, L.J. *If You Give A Mouse A Cookie*. HarperCollins Children's Books, 1985. ISBN 0060245867

Activity 21
Phonemic Awareness & Phonics
Segmentation

Goal

Students will be able to orally segment words into separate phonemes.

Area of Study

Language Arts

Interactive Writing Type

Negotiation

Resources

Discussions to stimulate writing questions that have a yes/no answer

Books about responsibility and classroom routines

Lessons

• Determine questions to be written interactively through classroom discussion about classroom routines.

• As short, one-syllable words are being written, demonstrate to the students how to segment each sound. Have them segment words aloud with you. The yes/no words are particularly effective words for children to begin with when learning the concept of segmentation.

Extensions

• Play segmentation games throughout the day to reinforce listening for individual phonemes. For example, ask the students to listen to you segment a word and determine the word: "I'm thinking of a word that sounds like this, /h/ /a/ /t/. What is it?"

• Create a literacy center that has short, familiar words that the children can read and then segment with a partner.

Additional Resources

Brown. M. *Arthur Makes the Team.* Little, Brown & Company, 1998. ISBN 0316115517

Ernst, L. *Stella Louella's Runaway Book.* Simon & Schuster Books for Young Readers, 1998. ISBN 0689818831

Keller, H. *That's Mine, Horace.* Greenwillow Books, 2000. ISBN 0688171591

Students slowly segmented words and listened for individual phonemes in this piece.

Activity 22
Phonemic Awareness & Phonics
Chunking and Blending

Goal
Students will look at text and identify parts or chunks of words that they recognize.

Area of Study
Language Arts

Interactive Writing Type
Negotiation

Resources
Books about rules that help develop a sense of community
Highlighter tape

Lessons

- Read aloud books at the beginning of the year as you work with the class to establish a community of learners.

- Determine together that the class will write procedures for literacy centers in the classroom. The written procedures will provide a resource throughout the year to foster independence.

- As the text is negotiated and written, encourage the students to listen for and to write larger chunks of words, rather than individual sounds. For example, when writing the word *listening*, students can identify the *–ing* as a chunk they know and write it as a unit.

- As the writing progresses, encourage the students to think of other words that contain the same chunk. The teacher may choose to write these words on the Magna Doodle to reinforce the visual similarity of the words.

- Once the text has been completed, read it again and highlight familiar chunks. Demonstrate to the children how they can use the chunks to read the word, by blending the sounds and chunks. You can return to these pieces throughout the year as new chunks are addressed in class.

Extensions

- Create a literacy center focusing on familiar word chunks. Students can search the interactive writing and shared reading pieces displayed in the room for words that contain a specified chunk.

- Choose a chunk that has been addressed during the interactive writing session. Ask the students to think of other

This interactive writing piece reinforces a routine and serves as a resource for using known word chunks.

words they know that contain that same chunk. Write the list interactively (for example, words that begin with *wh-*). Display this list of words in the classroom and use it as a resource during interactive writing lessons and independent writing.

Additional Resources

Howe, J. *I Wish I Were A Butterfly*. Harcourt Brace & Company, 1994. ISBN 0152380132

Myers, C. *Wings*. Scholastic, Inc., 2000. ISBN 0590033778

Weiss, G., and Thiele, B. *What A Wonderful World*. Simon & Schuster Children's, 1995. ISBN 068980087

Activity 23
Phonemic Awareness & Phonics
Root Words

Goal
Students will recognize root words, prefixes, and suffixes.

Areas of Study
Language Arts, Science

Interactive Writing Type
Negotiation

Resources
Books and other resources about living things
Highlighter tape
Magna Doodle

Lessons

- Provide many literacy experiences throughout a unit of study about living things, including read aloud and shared reading experiences.

- Engage the students in a nonfiction writing piece about living things. Guide them to use the knowledge they have gained during the unit of study as they negotiate text.

- During negotiation, the teacher will be aware of any words that contain root words. The teacher may suggest words that contain root words during the negotiation.

- Introduce the concept of a root word during the interactive writing.

- Show the students how to use a known root word to make new words by adding prefixes and suffixes. Use a Magna Doodle to demonstrate how simple known words such as *play* can be used to write more difficult words such as *replay*. Explain that this strategy can be used to write many words.

- Discuss the way the spellings of some words change when suffixes are added; for example, *baby* to *babies*.

- When the text is complete, use the piece as part of a shared reading lesson. Have the students locate the words containing root words. Then use the highlighter tape to highlight only the root word.

Extensions

- Create a literacy center that allows students to search for words containing root words. Students become "Root Word Detectives" as they read text on display in the classroom. As

After writing a definition of *living things*, second grade students highlighted the root words

they locate words containing root words, they can add these to a class resource list. This list can then become a basis for a sorting activity in which the students sort words based on common root words, prefixes, or suffixes.

- Expand this study of root words by discussing the meanings of common prefixes and/or suffixes; for example, *re-* means to do again.

Additional Resources

Herriot, J. *James Herriot's Treasury for Children*. St. Martin's Press, Inc., 1992. ISBN 0152018980

Kalman, B. *What is a Living Thing?* Crabtree Publishing Company, 1998. ISBN 0865058792

Ryder, J. *Each Living Thing*. Harcourt, 2000. ISBN 0152018980

Schimmel, S. *Dear Children of the Earth (A Letter from Home)*. Creative Publishing International, Inc., 1994. ISBN 1559712252

Activity 24
Phonemic Awareness & Phonics
Sounds in Sequence

Goal
Students will say words slowly and listen for sounds in sequence.

Area of Study
Language Arts

Interactive Writing Type
Transcription

Resources
Mother Goose book

Lessons

- Read aloud the poem "Hickory Dickory Dock" many times. Encourage the children to join in and recite the poem with you. Act out the poem with props.

- Once the children have memorized the poem, determine together that the class will write the poem.

- As each word is written, have the students say the word slowly and listen for the sounds in the word. Use the following prompts to help the students focus their attention on the sequence of the sounds in each word: "What sound do you hear first?" "What sound do you hear next?" and "What sound do you hear last?" If the students are naming sounds out of sequence, say, "That's right, that sound is in this word, but there is another sound before that sound. Say it again, and listen for the sound you hear first."

- Continue to write each word of the text. Remember, the students do not need to write each of the sounds contained in the word; the teacher may add the spelling for those sounds not heard.

Extensions

- Write other nursery rhymes interactively, and again focus on listening for sounds in sequence.

- During independent writing, encourage the students to slowly say the words they want to write, and listen for the sounds in sequence. Assist those students who are having trouble.

Additional Resources
Beaton, C. *Mother Goose Remembers*. Barefoot Books, Inc., 2000. ISBN 1841480738

The students slowly said the word *struck*. They were able to hear the initial /s/, the /r/, and the final /k/. The students wrote letters to represent those sounds, while the teacher wrote the letters *t*, *u* and *c*.

Hague, M. *Mother Goose (A Collection of Classic Nursery Rhymes)*. Henry Holt and Company, 1984. ISBN 0805002146

Lang, S. *Sylvia Lang's Mother Goose*. Chronicle Books, 1999. ISBN 0811820882

Sabuda, R. *The Movable Mother Goose*. Simon & Schuster Children's, 1999. ISBN 0689811926

Activity 25
Phonemic Awareness & Phonics
Analogy

Goal
Students will use words they already know to help them read and spell new words.

Area of Study
Language Arts, Science

Interactive Writing Type
Negotiation

Resources
Books about plants
Seeds of various vegetables
An area to plant a garden

Lessons

- As part of a unit of study on the life cycle of plants, read aloud a variety of books on the topic to build background knowledge. As a class activity, plant some seeds in a garden.

- Discuss the various steps involved in planting the garden. Determine together that the class will list these steps as directions for *How to Grow a Garden.*

- As the text is negotiated and written, look for opportunities to use words that will address the spelling strategy of analogy. For example, the students can write the word *seed* by thinking of a word that is already known to them, such as *see.* Teach the students that if they already know the word *seed* they can easily figure out how to write the word *need*, by using the rime of *–eed* and changing the first sound. Knowing the part, *sh*, will help students spell this same part in *sunshine* and *radish.*

- Remind the students throughout the writing that they can use words they know to help them spell words they do not know.

Extensions

- Address the use of analogy again during shared reading of the interactive writing piece, this time as a way to read a new word. Read other texts that have words that are displayed on the word wall or are similar to the students' names. Ask the students to think of words they know that are similar to the chosen word. For example, if the teacher highlights the word *choose*, the students may notice that the word starts like the name *Charity* or has the same spelling pattern *-oo* that is in the known word *too.*

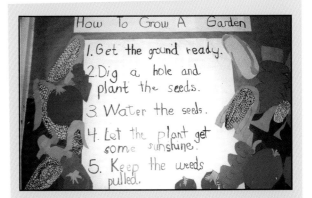

First grade children learned about words and parts of words that helped them write new words on a garden piece.

- Create a literacy center that focuses on analogy. The students will perform a word search. They will search the room for words that are similar to a designated word, such as *like.* They can then sort the words by similarities. For example, students can find words that have the initial *l* sound, words with an *–ike* spelling pattern, or words with a vowel-consonant-silent *e* spelling pattern

Additional Resources

Carle, E. *The Tiny Seed.* Simon & Schuster Children's, 1991. ISBN 0887080154

Cole, J., and Deger, B. *The Magic School Bus Plants Seeds: A Book About How Living Things Grow.* Scholastic, Inc., 1995. ISBN 0590222961

Ehlert, L. *Planting a Rainbow.* Harcourt, 1991. ISBN 0152626107

Gibbons, G. *From Seed to Plant.* Holiday House, Inc., 1991. ISBN 0823408728

Activity 26
Phonemic Awareness & Phonics
High Frequency Words

Goal
Students will learn to read and spell high frequency words.

Area of Study
Language Arts

Interactive Writing Type
Negotiation

Resources
Previous interactive writing pieces
Familiar shared reading pieces

Lessons

- To reinforce the spelling and availability of high frequency words in the classroom, ask the students to think of as many two-letter words as possible.

- Interactively write words the students can readily recall.

- Encourage the students to use the room as a resource by looking at previously written interactive pieces and familiar shared reading for two-letter words. Interactively write words found and add to the list.

- Read and reread the list to help with fluency and word recognition. Emphasize that these words should now be spelled correctly in their own individual writings and that these words will be posted as an additional resource.

- Add new words to the list as they become apparent to the students through other interactive writing and shared reading.

Extensions
- Using Wikki Stix, have the students go around the room and find other two-letter words to highlight during literacy center time.

- Design bingo type games, using the two-letter words written so the students can have additional practice reading these words.

Additional Resources
Falwell, C. *Word Wizard*. Houghton Mifflin Company, 1998. ISBN 0395855802

Prelutsky, J. *A Pizza the Size of the Sun*. Greenwillow Books, 1996. ISBN 0688132359

Wood, A. *The Napping House*. Harcourt Brace & Company, 1984. ISBN 0152567089

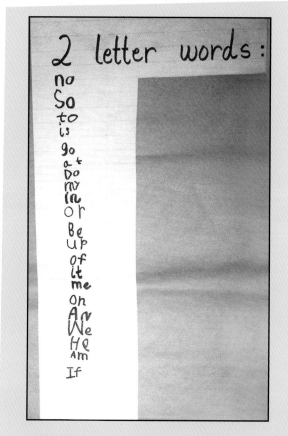

This picture shows the beginning of a list containing two-letter words.

Activity 27
Phonemic Awareness & Phonics
High Frequency Words

Goal
Students will learn to spell and read high frequency words.

Area of Study
Language Arts

Interactive Writing Type
Transcription

Resources
High interest texts of poetry that contain repeated use of targeted high frequency words
Highlighter tape

Lessons

- Read aloud selections of poetry and focus on one poem that the students particularly enjoy.

- Engage students in an interactive writing of the poem. Since the text does not have to be negotiated, the teacher and students are free to concentrate on specific high frequency words.

- As targeted high frequency words come up in the text, point them out as words the students will see all the time when they are reading. Explain that this is why it is important for them to learn to read and spell these words quickly and easily.

- Teach the students how to learn to spell and read a new word. First, have them look at the correct spelling and form a mental picture of the word. Then, have them write the word in the air while spelling it aloud several times. Have the students close their eyes, visualize the word, write the word in the air, and check the spelling against the correct spelling in the interactive writing text.

- Explain that the students may use the same procedure when learning to spell any other word.

- After completing the writing, return to the text and highlight the targeted high frequency word as many times as it occurs in the text with colored highlighter tape.

- Encourage the students to return to the piece often in order to help make connections to the word and see it used in context.

Here is a first grade transcription of the poem "I Like Bugs." The class learned the word *like* while writing this piece interactively.

Extensions

- Create a literacy center that allows the students to search for and write high frequency words. Have them read the text that is on display in the room and search for a targeted high frequency word. Have them write the word each time they locate it in a piece of text to reinforce correct spelling.

- Rewrite the poem on sentence strips and cut the words apart. As a class, rebuild the poem in a pocket chart and reread it. Point out the high frequency word and show the children how to use this known word to self-monitor when they are writing.

- Create a word wall in the classroom. Add high frequency and high utility words to the wall. Use the word wall as a reference during interactive writing and encourage students to use this resource during independent writing.

Additional Resources
Kennedy, X. J., and Kennedy, D. *Talking Like the Rain: A Read-to-Me Book of Poems*. Little, Brown & Company, 1992. ISBN 0316488895

Opie, I. A. *My Very First Mother Goose*. Candlewick Press, 1996. ISBN 1564026205

Prelutsky, J. *Ride A Purple Pelican*. William Morrow & Co., 1997. ISBN 0688156258

Sendak, M. *Chicken Soup with Rice: A Book of Months*. HarperCollins Children's Books, 1990. ISBN 006443253X

Activity 28
Phonemic Awareness & Phonics
Spelling Patterns

Goal
Students will recognize and identify words with common spelling patterns.

Areas of Study
Language Arts, Science

Interactive Writing Type
Transcription

Resources
Enlarged text of "Star Light, Star Bright"
Magna Doodle
Wikki Stix

Lessons
- Use the poem "Star Light, Star Bright" as a shared reading piece, in conjunction with a unit of study about the solar system. Reread the piece often, until the students can recite the poem from memory.

- Determine that the class will rewrite the poem from memory, without looking at the poster, so that the students can pay close attention to the sounds they hear in the words.

- During the writing, take time to discuss the -ight spelling pattern that occurs in four different words in the poem.

- Use the Magna Doodle. Demonstrate for the children how the word light can be changed to a new word by simply changing the first letter: night, sight. Write the new words on the Magna Doodle to visually show the common spelling pattern.

- When the writing is completed, return to the piece and underline the words containing the spelling pattern, using Wikki Stix.

Extensions
- Shrink the interactive writing on a copy machine and make a copy of the poem for each student. This poem can be added to an individual collection of poems for each student. Allow the students to read from their poetry books during independent reading or literacy centers.

- Select additional shared reading pieces that contain words with the -ight spelling pattern. Have the children search for and highlight those words.

Additional Resource
Rock, L. *I Wish Tonight*. Good Books, 1999. ISBN 156148315X

Students decorated this interactive writing piece by tracing and cutting their own stars.

Activity 29
Phonemic Awareness & Phonics
Blends, Digraphs, Diphthongs, and Vowels

Goal
Students will identify words with specified phonic skills.

Areas of Study
Language Arts, Mathematics

Interactive Writing Type
Transcription

Resources
Variety of counting books
Magna Doodle
Highlighter tape

Lessons
- Read aloud a variety of counting books.

- Choose one book that the students particularly enjoy and determine that the writing will list each of the items from the story in numerical order. The students will review number words and counting skills while working on a specific phonic skill.

- As the piece is being created, emphasize the phonic skill determined as the teaching focus for this writing session. For example, if digraphs are the focus, direct language to that phonic element. "What two letters make the sound /th/ in the word *thought*?"

- As words that contain these sounds are written, ask the students to brainstorm other words that contain those same sounds. Write the list of brainstormed words on a Magna Doodle and underline the common letters.

- On subsequent days, return to the interactive writing piece, rereading it as a shared reading piece. Highlight the different digraphs, using colored highlighter tape. Again ask the students to brainstorm lists of words that contain the same sound. Use interactive writing to write their ideas as a list.

- Post the lists created in the classroom and use them as resources for future writing activities.

Extensions
- Create a literacy center focusing on digraphs or any phonic element addressed during interactive writing. Have the children search the available interactive writing pieces, shared reading pieces, or independent reading selections for words with the

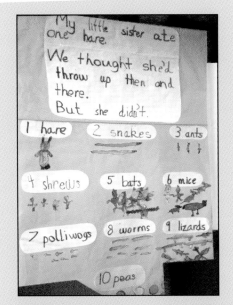

Students practiced counting skills while also learning about digraphs using this favorite piece.

selected phonic element. Have them copy any words they find and then read them to a partner.

- Use the text from the interactive writing to create a class book. Allow the students to illustrate the book.

- Select additional shared reading pieces containing the same phonic element being addressed. The students can locate new words to add to their lists.

Additional Resources
Grossman, B. *My Little Sister Ate One Hare*. Crown Publishers, Inc., 1996. ISBN 0517596008

Lesser, C. *SPOTS Counting Creatures from Sky to Sea*. Harcourt Brace & Company, 1999. ISBN 0152006664

Peek, M. *ROLLOVER! A Counting Song*. Houghton Mifflin Company, 1981. ISBN 039529438X

Root, P. *One Duck Stuck*. Candlewick Press, 1998. ISBN 0763603341

Sierra, J. *Counting Crocodiles*. Harcourt Brace & Company, 1997. ISBN 0152001921

Activity 30
Phonemic Awareness & Phonics
Alliteration

Goal
Students will demonstrate understanding of alliteration by writing sentences with a variety of words beginning with the same sound.

Area of Study
Language Arts

Interactive Writing Type
Negotiation

Resources
Books that illustrate the use of alliteration

Lessons

- Read aloud a variety of books that contain multiple examples of alliteration.

- While reading aloud, ask the students to listen to the sounds at the beginning of the words chosen by the author. Ask them to describe what they notice, leading them to discover that many words and phrases begin with the same sound.

- Suggest writing sentences with alliteration, using the students' names in the class.

- Review the concepts of adjectives and adverbs while negotiating sentences that illustrate the concept of alliteration.

- As each sentence is completed, allow time for the students to discuss ideas for the illustration that would add to the message.

- Continue writing the piece over several days so that all the students' names can be included.

- As illustrations are completed, compile the pages into a big book for all to enjoy in the class library.

Extensions

- Type and duplicate the text that was interactively written so each student has an individual copy of the book.

- Create a literacy center that encourages students to write a small play script using alliteration and present it to the class.

Here is an example from the class book using alliteration.

Additional Resources

Base, G. *Animalia*. Harry N. Abrams, Inc., 1987. ISBN 0810918684

Estes, K. *The Silly A B Seas*. Greene Bark Press, 1997. ISBN 188085127X

Gallop, J. *Silly Animal ABC's*. Courage Books, Inc., 1999. ISBN 0762405066

Grover, M. *The Accidental Zucchini*. Harcourt, 1993. ISBN 01530335358

Lyne, A. *A My Name Is...* Whispering Coyote Press, 1997. ISBN 1879085402

Shelby, A. *Potluck*. Barton, Press, Inc., 1994. ISBN 053107045X

Activity 31
Written Language Conventions
Punctuation

Goal
Students will identify different types of punctuation, discuss proper usage, and utilize the punctuation correctly in a new text.

Area of Study
Language Arts

Interactive Writing Type
Negotiation

Resources
Shared reading text that has a question and answer format
Highlighter tape

Lessons

- Choose a familiar shared reading text that features a question and answer format.

- Have the class reread the text fluently. Draw attention to the punctuation, and discuss how punctuation helps readers to read text fluently and with expression.

- Prompt the students to locate and identify different types of punctuation used in the shared reading piece. Guide the discussion about the different purposes for the types of punctuation used in the text.

- Discuss the difference between telling and asking types of sentences and determine the punctuation used when asking a question.

- Highlight the question marks in the text, using colored highlighter tape.

- Negotiate and interactively write the definition of a question.

- Expand on the initial discussion of the use of question marks by choosing additional shared reading pieces that contain questions. Prompt the students to notice that questions often begin with particular words, such as *why* and *who*. Add these words to the definition of a question.

Extensions
- Read aloud a variety of books containing riddles. Write some riddles interactively, focusing on questions. Then encourage the students to write riddles independently. Assemble the riddles in a class book.

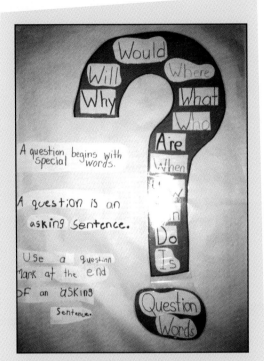

A group of students interactively wrote this definition of a question. They were then able to refer to this definition as a resource when writing independently.

- Create a literacy center that allows the students to practice their use of question marks. On sentence strips, write a variety of sentences that require periods or question marks. Laminate the strips. Students may then read the sentences, decide on the correct punctuation, and add that punctuation.

Additional Resources
Ferris, K. *The Kids' Question and Answer Book*. Putnam Publishing Group, 1988. ISBN 0448192217

Madgwick, W. *Questions and Answers (Inventions)*. Kingfisher Publications, 2000. ISBN 0753453118

Stock, G. *The Kids' Book of Questions*. Workman Publishing Company, Inc., 1988. ISBN 0894806319

Activity 32
Written Language Conventions
Capitalization

Goal
Students will learn to capitalize proper nouns.

Areas of Study
Language Arts, Social Studies

Interactive Writing Type
Transcription

Resources
Variety of nonfiction books about rainforests
Map of the world

Lessons
• Read aloud a variety of books about rainforests to build the students' background knowledge.

• Create a map of the world. Use interactive writing to label the world's existing rainforests.

• As continents and countries are labeled, discuss capitalization rules for proper nouns.

• Provide examples of proper and common nouns to help the students understand the difference. Begin by making a connection to their names as examples of proper nouns. Use known words such as *boy* and *girl* to illustrate common nouns .

Extensions
• Use interactive writing to record the rules the class has learned for capitalization. Add to the list as new rules are learned. Include examples of each rule. This resource can then be displayed in the classroom and used by the students during interactive and independent writing.

• Create a literacy center, focusing on proper and common nouns. Do not capitalize proper nouns. The students can then work together to sort the nouns and edit for proper capitalization.

• Look for evidence in independent writing indicating that the students are capitalizing proper nouns appropriately.

Additional Resources
Baker, L. *Life in the Rainforest*. Scholastic, Inc., 1993.
ISBN 0590461311

Forsyth, A. *How Monkeys Make Chocolate: Foods* and *Medicines from the Rainforests*. Firefly Books, Ltd., 1995.
ISBN 1895688450

Pratt, K. *A Walk in the Rainforest*. Dawn Publications, 1992.
ISBN 1878265997

Students used this map of the world to learn about the capitalization of proper nouns.

Activity 33
Written Language Conventions
Spelling and Word Analysis

Goal
Students will analyze unknown words using spelling patterns.

Areas of Study
Language Arts, Science

Interactive Writing Type
Negotiation

Resources
Variety of nonfiction books about insects
Shared reading texts about insects
Variety of media about insects; films, posters, slides
Shape of an insect drawn on large poster paper

Lessons
- As part of a unit of study on living things, immerse the students in a variety of media about insects.

- Engage the students in a discussion of the physical attributes and characteristic body parts of insects.

- Display a large poster of each insect studied. Locate insect body parts and label them interactively.

- As each word is written, help the students analyze each word, demonstrating how to use what they know about words to help them write new, unknown words. For example, a multi-syllabic word can be broken into syllables. Each syllable can then be analyzed and worked out separately. For example, *antennae* can be broken into three syllables, which are then analyzed separately. The first syllable may be described as the *-an* chunk, the second as an example of onset and rime from the known name, *Ben,* and the third may be discussed in terms of its Latin origins.

- Encourage the students to think about each of the words and help them think of a variety of strategies for spelling those words accurately. Strategies that students could use include: stretching words and recording sounds heard, use of onset and rime, analogy, and word origin.

Extensions
- Create a literacy center in which students sort labels by spelling patterns. Students may also generate or search for other words that contain that same spelling pattern.

- Have the students independently write about insects, using the posters as resources.

Additional Resources
Florian, D. *Insectlopedia.* Harcourt Brace & Company, 1998. ISBN 0152013067

Hepworth, C., and Paulsen, N. *Bug Off!: A Swarm of Insect Words.* Putnam Publishing Group, 1998. ISBN 0399226400

Parker, S. *It's an Ant's Life (My Story of Life in the Nest).* Reader's Digest Children's Publishing, Inc., 1999. ISBN 1575843153

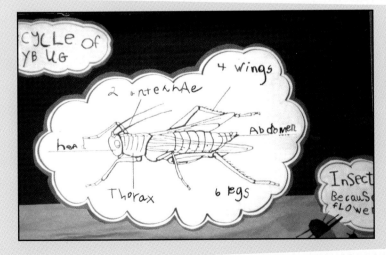

This is one example of a first grade unit on grasshoppers. Grasshoppers and other insects were studied during a four-week period.

Activity 34
Written Language Conventions
Spelling and Word Analysis

Goal
Students will analyze unknown words, using spelling patterns.

Areas of Study
Language Arts, Mathematics

Interactive Writing Type
Negotiation

Resources
Variety of number books

Lessons

- Read aloud a variety of number and counting books. Look for picture books that have stories featuring the numbers 1-20 and then proceed to count by tens to 100.

- Encourage the students to interactively write a list of number words that will serve as a resource in the classroom.

- Number words have many irregular spelling patterns. There will need to be lengthy discussions about the use of spelling strategies and word analysis skills as the words are interactively written.

- Direct the students to think of strategies that will help them figure out unknown words. Use questions such as, "What do you know about this word?" or "What strategy would be most helpful in thinking about how to spell this word?" Strategies would include: stretching words and recording the sounds heard, use of onset and rime, analogy, breaking words into syllables, and word origin.

Extensions

- Create a literacy center to reinforce correct spelling of number words. Students can use magnetic letters to spell the words, using the interactively written list as a resource.

- Allow the students to illustrate individual number books.

Additional Resources
McGrath, B. *The Cheerios Counting Book.* Scholastic, Inc., 1998. ISBN 0590683578

Pallotta J. *Reese's Pieces Count by Fives.* Scholastic, Inc., 2000. ISBN 0439135206

Ryan, P.M. *One Hundred Is a Family.* Hyperion Books for Children, 1994. ISBN 1562826727

Wells, R. *Emily's First 100 Days of School.* Hyperion Books for Children, 2000. ISBN 0786805072

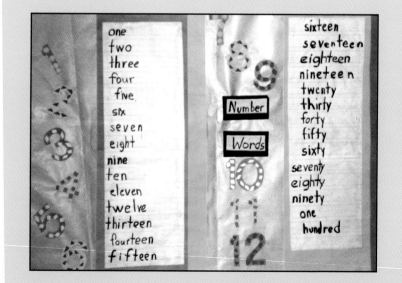

This attractive display of numerals and number words remains in a visible area in the classroom so students have access to it.

Activity 35
Written Language Conventions
Sentence Structure

Goal

Students will construct sentences using appropriate language structure.

Areas of Study

Language Arts, Mathematics

Interactive Writing Type

Negotiation

Resources

Read aloud books dealing with money
Math coin manipulatives

Lessons

- Read aloud books that have a story line about money.

- Provide opportunities for the students to discuss what they know about money and experiences they have had with money.

- Provide opportunities for the students to manipulate coins and role-play different situations that deal with the use of money.

- Engage the students in an interactive writing piece about money. As they share ideas orally, participate in the negotiation by taking their ideas and modifying them so that they reflect proper grammar and language structure. As part of the negotiation, discuss the difference between the informal way we speak and the more formalized book language we encounter in print.

- During the negotiation, use prompts such as, "To make it sound right, let's say it this way" or "In English we say…" or "In a book, it might sound like this…" Pay attention to sentence structure while formulating a clear message.

- Use similar sentence structure throughout the piece to enable the students to become more familiar with the use of the new structure.

Extensions

- Engage the students in other interactive pieces that use the same sentence structure. It is helpful to begin with simple sentence structure and practice it often before moving on to more complicated structures.

- Provide copies of paper coins. Give the students opportunities to use the coins to write and solve word problems about money.

- Create a literacy center with a restaurant theme. The students may read menus, copy orders, figure out the cost of meals, and pay with play money.

Additional Resources

Brisson, P. *Benny's Pennies*. Bantam Doubleday Dell Books for Young Readers, 1995. ISBN 0440410169

Hoban, T. *26 Letters and 99 Cents*. William Morrow & Co., 1995. ISBN 068814389X

McMillan, B. *Jelly Beans For Sale*. Scholastic, 1996. ISBN 0590865846

Murphy, S. *The Penny Pot*. HarperCollins Publishers, Inc., 1999. ISBN 0060276061

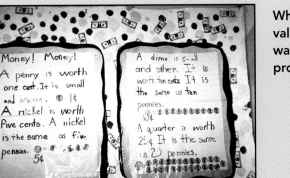

While learning about the value of coins, this class was also able to discuss proper sentence structure.

Activity 36
Written Language Conventions
Sentence Structure

Goal
Students will construct complex sentences.

Areas of Study
Language Arts, Science

Interactive Writing Type
Negotiation

Resources
Variety of read aloud, nonfiction books about endangered animals

Variety of media about endangered animals; posters, films, slides

Lessons
• Read aloud many books about endangered animals, especially studying in depth about animals of particular interest to the students.

• Look at the students' independent writing for evidence of actual use of complex sentence structure. Based on need, begin instruction of merging two simple sentences to form a more complex one.

• Share information about knowledge of endangered animals. During the negotiation process, the teacher talks explicitly about how to organize multiple ideas into one complex sentence.

• Demonstrate blending sentences by using ideas from two or three students and combining them to make one sentence.

• Demonstrate how connecting words such as *because, and,* or other conjunctions brings two like ideas together into one complete sentence.

• Continue writing other facts about additional endangered animals until the students verbalize compound, complex sentences.

Extensions
• Paint pictures of endangered animals and habitats to go with the writing.

• Interactively write additional pieces about other endangered animals, with an emphasis on writing complex sentences.

• Provide opportunities for students to write independently on the topic.

Additional Resources
Burton, B. *Endangered, Mammals!* Gareth Stevens Audio, 1996. ISBN 083681424X

Irvine, G. *Endangered Species At The San Diego Zoo.* Scholastic, 1990. ISBN 0590468642

Kennedy, T. *Bringing Back the Animals.* Scholastic, Inc., 1991. ISBN 0590463861

Smith, R. *Sea Otter Rescue.* Scholastic, Inc., 1990. ISBN 059046213X

Wright, A. *Will We Miss Them?: Endangered Animals.* Charlesbridge Publishing Inc., 1993. ISBN 0881064882

The California Condor is endangered because people have killed them, people have taken their homes, and people have poisoned them.

The function of the word *because* **spurred a lively discussion about the complexities of sentences that would be written by a group of children.**

Activity 37
Written Language Conventions
Grammar

Goal
Students will understand and use correct grammar when writing.

Areas of Study
Language Arts, Mathematics

Interactive Writing Type
Transcription

Resources
A variety of mathematics books, focusing on subtraction
Art supplies, Velcro

Lessons

- Read aloud several mathematics books that have rhythm and repeated phrases in order to find one that the students particularly enjoy. Reread the book many times so that they become familiar with the story line and sentence structure of the book.

- Choose different sequences from the story to dramatize. This will reinforce the concept of subtraction while allowing the students to internalize the language of the book.

- Choose a portion of the text to write interactively. Since grammar is the focus of the lesson, find sentences in the book that have different verb tenses.

- Write the text exactly as it was written in the book. Remember, this is not a copying task. During interactive writing of an existing text, the students will analyze words.

- While writing, discuss the proper use of verb tenses in each sentence. Encourage the students to think of other sentences that use the same verb or verb tense.

- Reread the interactive writing many times as a class.

Extensions

- As part of a literacy center, create art that mimics the original text and can be manipulated by the students. The students' paintings can be displayed along with the interactive writing text. Attach Velcro to the backs of the paintings to enable the students to dramatize the story while rereading the text.

- Create individual books for the students, using the same text.

- Encourage the students to write an innovation of the story during independent writing.

This interactive writing can be read over and over again during shared reading and as a literacy center. This chart easily became a class favorite.

Additional Resources

Cato, S. *Subtraction*. Lerner Publishing Group, 1999. ISBN 1575053187

Leedy, L. *Subtraction Action*. Holiday House, Inc., 2000. ISBN 082341454X

McCourt, L. *The Candy Counting Book: Delicious Ways to Add and Subtract*. Bridgewater Books, 1999. ISBN 0816763291

Toft, K. M. *one less fish*. Charlesbridge Publishing, Inc., 1998. ISBN 0881063223

Activity 38
Written Language Conventions
Parts of Speech

Goal
Students will recognize and identify parts of speech.

Area of Study
Language Arts

Interactive Writing Type
Negotiation

Resources
Shared readings, poems, and short stories in a variety of genre

Lessons
- Select a shared reading piece that has many examples of a particular part of speech.

- Focus the students' attention on one part of speech at a time. Read the text together and help them identify the appropriate words.

- Provide many opportunities for the students to learn about each part of speech through the context of many texts.

- During subsequent rereadings, encourage the students to demonstrate understanding by using movement activities. They might act out verbs or clap nouns.

- Negotiate a class definition of a part of speech you have been learning about. Interactively write the class constructed definition and display this in the classroom as a reference.

- Go through this same process while the students learn other parts of speech.

Extensions
- Create a literacy center that allows students to practice identifying parts of speech. They can search through familiar shared readings or interactive writing to locate specified parts of speech. These can be recorded on sheets of paper.

- Challenge the students to read a passage of text from a content area textbook and list all the words of a particular part of speech.

- During independent writing, encourage the students to use what they have learned to make their writing more interesting.

There is no doubt that this class of third graders knows the definition and usage of nouns, adverbs, and adjectives.

Additional Resources

Cleary, B. *A Mink, a Fink, a Skating Rink: What is a Noun?* Lerner Publishing Group, 2000. ISBN 1575054175

Heller, R. *Up, Up, and Away: A Book about Adverbs.* Putnam Publishing Group, 1998. ISBN 0698116631

Heller, R. *Many Luscious Lollipops: A Book about Adjectives.* Putnam Publishing Group, 1991. ISBN 0448031515

Katz, B. *25 Great Grammar Poems and Activities.* Scholastic, Inc., 1999. ISBN 0590983652

Maizels, J., and Petty, K. *The Amazing Pop-Up Grammar Book.* Penguin, USA, 1996. ISBN 0525455809

Activity 39
Written Language Conventions
Word Usage

Goal
Students will select and extend vocabulary choices.

Areas of Study
Language Arts, Science

Interactive Writing Type
Negotiation

Resources
Nonfiction and fiction books about rainbows

Lessons
- Read aloud a variety of books about rainbows.

- Encourage the students to come up with many words that describe rainbows. Talk about how authors use descriptive words to help the reader visualize the topic and make it more interesting.

- Point out that many words may mean almost the same thing. For example, *pretty*, *beautiful*, *cute*, and *attractive* have similar meanings.

- Help the students to negotiate sentences that describe rainbows. During the negotiation, prompt them to think of interesting words to use in their description. Help them to think of alternative choices for words in order to expand their vocabulary.

Extensions
- Create a literacy center that allows students to practice thinking of alternative word choices. Write sentences on sentence strips and circle specific words. The students can copy the sentences and replace the circled words with words that mean the same thing. Encourage them to write several sentences on each strip.

- Share riddles with the students. Encourage them to interactively write riddles that use interesting words to describe the colors of the rainbow. For example, "Red is bright and shiny and can be flaming hot. Red is a ___."

- Use interactive writing to make a special word bank with words that can be used to describe rainbows.

Additional Resources
Cole, J., and Degen, B. *The Magic School Bus Makes a Rainbow: A Book About Color.* Scholastic, Inc., 1997. ISBN 0590922513

Fowler, A. *All the Colors of the Rainbow.* Children's Press, 1998. ISBN 0516208012

Hanel, W. *The Gold at the End of the Rainbow.* North-South Books, 1997. ISBN 155858692X

The class had an interesting discussion about word usage as they described a rainbow.

Activity 40
Phonemic Awareness & Phonics
Irregular Words

Goal
Students will become familiar with homophones.

Area of Study
Language Arts

Interactive Writing Type
Negotiation

Resources
Read aloud books and shared readings with multiple examples of homophones

Lessons

- Choose shared readings that have multiple examples of homophones. Encourage discussion throughout the reading, particularly the questions and comments about homophones.

- Ask the students to locate words in the text that sound alike but are spelled differently. Tell them that these words are called homophones.

- Negotiate a definition for the word *homophone* and write it interactively.

- During shared reading, search for examples of homophones and highlight them. Use these to begin a list of pairs of homophones. This list will serve as a resource that can be readily accessed by students when they are reading and writing.

- Interactively write a sentence that uses several homophones. Talk to the students about the types of illustrations that would help them to understand the meanings of each of the homophones used.

- Allow the students to Illustrate the sentences.

- Continue to add to the homophone list over time.

Extensions

- Divide the students into pairs and give each pair a set of homophones from the interactively written list. The students will write and illustrate sentences of their own, patterned after the interactive writing.

- Create a concentration type game in which students match homophone pairs.

- Create a Pear-Pair Tree. Construct a bare tree on a bulletin

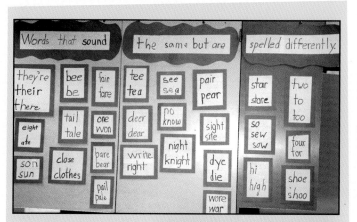

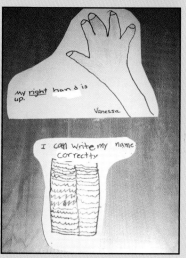

A third grade class defines and lists many homophones.

To further understanding of homophones, this class-made book used homophone sets in sentences.

board in the classroom. Make blank pear-shaped pieces of yellow construction paper. Have the students work together to create pairs of homophones to write on the pear shapes. Place the pairs of homophone pears on the tree.

Additional Resources

Ghigna, C. *See the Yak Yak*. Random House, Inc., 1999. ISBN 0679891358

Gwynne, F. *A Chocolate Moose For Dinner*. Simon & Schuster Children's, 1988. ISBN 0671667416

Maestro, G. *What's Mite Might?* Houghton Mifflin, 1986. ISBN 0899194354

Ziefert, H. *Night, Knight!* Houghton Mifflin, 1997. ISBN 0395851602

Activity 41
Phonemic Awareness & Phonics
Onomatopoeia

Goal

Students will recognize words that imitate the sounds associated with the objects or actions they describe.

Area of Study

Language Arts

Interactive Writing Type

Negotiation

Resources

Read aloud books that demonstrate use of onomatopoeia

Lessons

- Read aloud books that contain examples of onomatopoeia (words that imitate the sounds associated with them or an action they refer to, such as *buzz*, *murmur*, and *klop*). The students will enjoy books that have repetitive, patterned text.

- Select books that have sounds made by animals.

- Point out the words the author used to describe sounds made by the animals in the story. Read these words and talk about the fact that they sound similar to the objects or actions they describe.

- Interactively write the words from the story that are examples of onomatopoeia.

- Encourage discussion about the definition of *onomatopoeia*.

- Brainstorm, negotiate, and interactively write other words that match this definition.

Extensions

- Design a literacy center that allows students to record examples of onomatopoeia. Provide speech bubbles for them to use when writing animal sounds.

- Create a set of books that use onomatopoeia for the students to read independently.

Additional Resources

Clements, A. *DOUBLE TROUBLE in Walla Walla*. Millbrook Press, 1997. ISBN 0761302751

Cronin, D. *Click, Clack, Moo Cows That Type*. Simon & Schuster Books for Young Readers, 2000. ISBN 0689832133

DeZutter, H. *Who Says A Dog Goes Bow-Wow?* Dell Publishing Company, 1997. ISBN 0440413389

Lewis, K. *Chugga-Chugga Choo-Choo*. Hyperion Books for Children, 1999. ISBN 0786804297

This is a first grade example of words generated for a display utilizing onomatopoeia.

Activity 42
Phonemic Awareness & Phonics
Contractions

Goal
Students will discuss the meaning and proper use of a variety of contractions.

Area of Study
Language Arts

Interactive Writing Type
Negotiation

Resources
Variety of books about friendship

Lessons

- Read aloud many books and engage the students in discussions about friendship.

- Invite the students to share ideas about the qualities of a good friend. Encourage them to think about each of their classmates' qualities. Use this discussion as the basis for an interactive writing piece.

- During the negotiation of the text, look for opportunities to use contractions. For example, if a student suggests, "Laurel is a good friend because she is patient," the teacher would affirm the response and then say, "We could also say it this way: Laurel is a good friend because she's patient." The teacher is now able to effectively discuss the meanings of different contractions and encourage the children's use of them meaningfully within context of the writing.

- Continue to write sentences about each student, encouraging the use of contractions during the negotiation.

Extensions

- Interactively write a definition of what makes a contraction. Include a list of commonly used contractions that can be posted and used as a resource in the classroom. Add to the list as students notice new contractions in their reading and writing.

- The students can work in pairs to write about each other's positive qualities, using the class interactive writing as a guideline.

- Create a literacy center that allows the students to practice their use of contractions. Write a variety of contractions with their partners on sentence strips (for example, *can't* and *cannot*). Students can then read the contractions, and match them with their corresponding phrase.

Additional Resources

Danzinger, P., and Martin, A. *P.S. Longer Letter Later*. Listening Library Inc., 1999. ISBN 0807280852

Johnson, T. *Amber on the Mountain*. Penguin Books, 1994. ISBN 0803712197

Parr, T. *The Best Friends Book*. Little, Brown & Company, 2000. ISBN 0316692018

Pfister, M. *The Rainbow Fish*. North-South Books, 1992. ISBN 1558580093

Silverstein, S. *The Giving Tree*. HarperCollins Children's Books, 1986. ISBN 0060256656

This second grade class enjoyed writing about their classmates. The interactive writing was eventually reformatted into a big book that students were able to revisit throughout the year.

Activity 43
Writing Process
Idea Development

Goal
Students will write detailed sentences that fully develop a topic.

Areas of Study
Language Arts, Science

Interactive Writing Type
Negotiation

Resources
Various nonfiction, read aloud books about bees

Lessons

- Read aloud a variety of books about bees to build the students' background knowledge.

- After each reading, ask the students to share the main idea or major facts learned from the text.

- Use the students' ideas to negotiate factual sentences. Throughout the negotiation, focus the students' attention on blending ideas to form sentences that are rich in information. Encourage them to write more than one sentence for each topic, in order to explain each idea more thoroughly.

- Write these sentences interactively.

Extensions

- As a class, sort the sentences by topic. Organize the sentences into paragraphs, adding topic sentences and concluding sentences.

- Type the interactive writing text and reproduce a copy for each student in the class. The students can then illustrate the text and use the interactive writing as a study guide for the topic of study.

Additional Resources

Cole J., and Deger, B. *The Magic School Inside a Beehive.* Scholastic, Inc., 1997. ISBN 0590257218

Gibbons, G. *The Honey Makers.* William Morrow & Co., 2000. ISBN 0688175317

High, L.O. *Beekeepers.* Boyds Mill Press, 1998. ISBN 156397486X

Hogan, P. *The Life Cycle of the Honeybee.* Raintree Steck-Vaughn Publishers, 1995. ISBN 0811481794

This is a third grade example of interactive writing in the area of science.

Activity 44
Writing Process
Text Organization

Goal
Students will learn to organize information, using a variety of formats.

Areas of Study
Language Arts, Science

Interactive Writing Type
Negotiation

Resources
Enlarged text of the Scientific Method
Materials needed to conduct several science experiments

Lessons
- Familiarize the students with the Scientific Method by engaging them in several science experiments.

- Explain that texts are organized in various ways to meet specific purposes. Science experiments are often recorded with a specific format and common vocabulary.

- As a shared reading, introduce an enlarged text displaying an example of the Scientific Method, along with definitions of key terms.

- Read the text together and apply key terms to the experiments previously done by the students in class.

- Choose one experiment to write about, using the Scientific Method format. During the negotiation, encourage the students to use the new vocabulary, such as *hypothesis* and *conclusion*.

Extensions
- Allow the students to perform their own experiments in cooperative groups and write about those experiments, using the proper format.

- During a school science fair, have the students explain their experiments orally to groups of visiting parents, using appropriate vocabulary.

In preparation for the annual science fair, the teacher helped students organize text into an appropriate format.

Additional Resources
Crews, N. *A High, Low, Near, Far, Loud, Quiet, Story.* Greenwillow Books, 1999. ISBN 0688167942

Minters, F. *Too Big, Too Small, Just Right.* Harcourt, 2001. ISBN 0152021574

Wilbur, R. *Runaway Opposites.* Harcourt, 1995. ISBN 0152587225

Activity 45
Writing Process
Text Organization

Goal
Students will learn a variety of ways to organize text for different purposes.

Areas of Study
Language Arts, Mathematics

Interactive Writing Type
Negotiation

Resources
Variety of read aloud books about money
Play or real money for manipulatives
Paper divided into graph format

Lessons
- Review coins by reading aloud books in which money and the value of money are discussed in both fiction and nonfiction stories.

- Use interactive writing to introduce a problem-solving strategy that uses text that has been organized into a chart format.

- Assist the students in constructing a chart that organizes information about coins. Decide together which attributes to label and write these interactively.

- Explain that a chart can help organize information and make it easier to find when specific information is needed. Order and arrange interactive writing text on the chart, with the students' assistance.

- Pose questions that require the students to access information from the chart. As they answer each question, have them point out the information on the chart that helped them answer that question. Then have them explain their thinking processes.

- Assist the students with locating information as needed.

Extensions
- Use interactive writing to create another chart about paper money, using the same organizational format.

- Use interactive writing to create story problems that require the students to refer to the chart they have created.

- Encourage the students to write their own story problems about money during independent writing or literacy centers. These may be compiled into a class book or become a basis for "Word Problem of the Day."

Additional Resources
Adams, B. *The Go-Around Dollar*. Simon Schuster Children's Publishing, 1992. ISBN 0027000311

Gill, S. *The Big Buck Adventure*. Charlesbridge Publishing, Inc., 2000. ISBN 0881062944

Kimmel, E. *Four Dollars and Fifty Cents*. Holiday House, Inc., 1998. ISBN 0823410242

Leedy, L. *Monster Money*. Holiday House, Inc., 1992. ISBN 0823409228

Wells, R. *BUNNY MONEY*. Penguin Putnam Books, 2000. ISBN 014056750X

A third and fourth grade class reviewed key concepts about coins and organized the information on this chart.

Activity 46
Writing Process
Outlining

Goal
Students will learn to organize ideas, using an outline format.

Areas of Study
Language Arts, Science

Interactive Writing Type
Negotiation

Resources
Variety of nonfiction texts about sea creatures

Lessons

- As part of a unit of study on the ocean, read aloud nonfiction texts about creatures who live in the deep sea.

- Explain that outlining is a way to organize information or ideas before beginning to write a paragraph or essay.

- Decide that the class will organize some of the information they have learned about various sea creatures, using an outline format. Choose a topic and write that topic as a title. Throughout the interactive writing, discuss outline format.

- Decide together which creatures the class will write about. Choose one to begin and write the name in the proper place for outline format.

- Ask the students to contribute facts they remember about the creature from the discussions. Help them to sort their ideas and record them, using interactive writing. Stress that an outline is a tool for organizing ideas and that these ideas do not need to be recorded in sentence format. Help them shorten ideas so they contain only key words or phrases.

- Throughout the interactive writing lesson, stress the format and organization of an outline. During the negotiation of each new portion of text, help the students to decide where to place the information in the outline, based on its content.

- Think aloud while sorting and categorizing the information in this manner so the students understand decision making.

- Choose a new creature and repeat the process. While supporting the students through the process, focus attention on outline format.

- Post the interactive writing in the classroom so the students can use it as a resource when writing other outlines.

Extensions

- Use the outline the class has written to interactively write a paragraph about each sea creature.

- Allow the students to work in pairs or independently to write their own outlines. Provide readings of short, high-interest text for them to read and outline. Provide paper that has an outline template to ensure that they use the proper format.

Additional Resources
Berger, M. *Dive! A Book of Deep-Sea Creatures*. Scholastic, 2000. ISBN 0439087473

Brown, A. *Amazing Sea Creatures*. Crabtree Publishing, 1997. ISBN 0865055610

Cerullo, M. *The Truth About Great White Sharks*. Chronicle Books, 2000. ISBN 0811824675

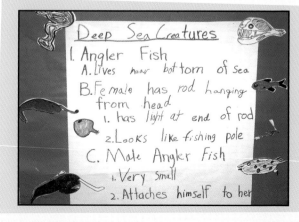

Students refer to this model when attempting to write their own outlines. This example is more meaningful than a commercially produced text because the students were actually involved in its construction.

Activity 47
Writing Process
Vocabulary and Word Choice

Goal

Students will learn new vocabulary that is tied to a content area and use that vocabulary appropriately when speaking and writing.

Areas of Study

Language Arts, Mathematics

Interactive Writing Type

Transcription

Resources

Three-dimensional shapes

Lessons

- Explore three-dimensional materials in mathematics.

- Describe shapes, using appropriate mathematical vocabulary.

- Sort and classify additional objects that students regularly see in their environment, using the same mathematical vocabulary.

- Identify and label the three-dimensional shapes, using interactive writing. Create a bulletin board that displays each of the labels, along with examples of each shape.

- Refer to the interactive writing often to ensure that the students will use the specialized vocabulary naturally and with understanding.

Extensions

- Use interactive writing to write definitions or descriptions of each three-dimensional shape. Post these in the room for the students to use as a resource.

- Use interactive writing to create stories, using the new vocabulary. The students' illustrations will match the text and show examples of three-dimensional shapes.

- Create a literacy center in which students can reread the label for each of the shapes and then sort other environmental items by shape.

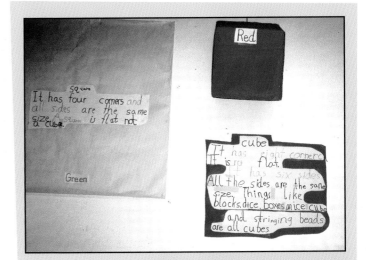

Students manipulate and read these sentences about shapes during literacy centers.

Additional Resources

Adler, D. *SHAPE UP!* Holiday House, Inc., 1998. ISBN 0823423462

Brumbeau, J. *The Quiltmaker's Gift*. Pfeifer-Hamilton Publishers, 1999. ISBN 1570251991

Burns, M. *The Greedy Triangle*. Scholastic, Inc., 1995. ISBN 0590489917

Friedman, A. *A Cloak For The Dreamer*. Scholastic, Inc., 1995. ISBN 0590489879

Activity 48
Writing Process
Concept Development

Goal
Students will determine the important facts about a topic in order to write a paragraph.

Areas of Study
Language Arts, Visual Arts

Interactive Writing Type
Negotiation

Resources
Books about artists
Biographies
Prints of artists' works

Lessons

- During a study of famous artists, immerse the students in the artists' works. Examine many examples from different artists and invite comments about the students' observations and interpretations.

- Decide to write a short biography about an artist whose works the students particularly enjoy. Review and brainstorm facts about the artist's life and style of art.

- During the negotiation, determine the most important facts that need to be included in the biography. The focus of this lesson is to help the students to determine important facts. Talk about which facts are the most important to include in a paragraph about this artist. Discuss what is important and interesting to include for an audience that knows little about the artist.

- Negotiate the exact text to be written and write it interactively.

Extensions

- Using the interactive writing as the beginning paragraph, the students can independently add text about the artist.

- Expand the visual arts study to include more artists and their work.

- Engage the students in an art lesson in which they mimic the artist's work.

Additional Resources

Bjork, C. *LINNEA In Monet's Garden.* Raben & Sjogren Publishers, 1985. ISBN 9129583144

Micklethwart, L. *I SPY (An Alphabet In Art).* Greenwillow Books, 1992. ISBN 0688116195

Stanley, D. *Leonardo da Vinci.* Morrow, 1996. ISBN 0688104371

Waldman, C. *The Starry Night.* Boyds Mill Press, Inc., 1999. ISBN 1563977362

This picture shows the combination of an art lesson and an interactive writing lesson as it was displayed in the classroom.

Activity 49
Writing Process
Concept Development

Goal
Students will develop the concept of estimation and write descriptive sentences.

Areas of Study
Language Arts, Mathematics

Interactive Writing Type
Negotiation

Resources
Large jar
2 - 4 sets of various contents for jar (marbles, candy, etc.)

Lessons

- As part of a unit of study in mathematics, prepare the students for an estimating task by discussing the purpose of estimating items.

- Set out a large jar filled with a set of like items. Ask each student to estimate the number of items in the jar. The teacher may record the estimates.

- On another day, fill the jar with items that are a different size than those used in the first lesson. As the students make new estimates, ask them to discuss their strategies for the new estimations.

- Again, count the contents of the jar and record the data on a graph. Repeat this process at least two more times.

- Analyze the graphed data and interactively write statements that describe the information displayed in the graph. As part of the discussion, encourage the students to review the types of strategies they used to refine their estimates.

- During the negotiation, encourage the use of mathematical terms. The students will increase concept knowledge through this dialogue, while developing strategies for future use when estimating.

Extensions

- Use interactive writing to list effective strategies used in estimating tasks.

- Use the estimation jar for other estimation and graphing tasks.

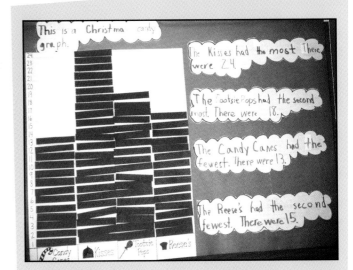

This Christmas candy graph looks delicious! Analyzing this data provided new mathematical vocabulary for a first grade class.

- Negotiate and interactively write questions for the students to use in surveying classmates on a specified topic. Allow them to gather data from the survey and record the data in a graph format.

Additional Resources

Barrett, J. *Cloudy With a Chance of Meatballs.* Simon & Schuster, 1978. ISBN 0689707495

Giff, P. *The Candy Corn Contest.* Bantam Doubleday Dell Books for Young Readers, 1984. ISBN 044041072X

McGrath, B. *More M & M's MATH.* Charlesbridge Publishing, Inc., 1998. ISBN 0881069949

Murphy, S. *BETCHA.* HarperCollins Children's Books, 1997. ISBN 0060267682

Activity 52
Writing Process
Paragraph Development

Goal
Students will learn to organize sentences into paragraphs.

Areas of Study
Language Arts, Mathematics

Interactive Writing Type
Negotiation

Resources
Read aloud books about time

Lessons

- Read aloud a book that reviews the concept of time. Clarify understanding throughout the reading.

- Decide with the students that the class will interactively write a paragraph that summarizes the information from the read aloud. Give the students a definition of a paragraph, so they understand the term.

- Have the students brainstorm key concepts from the text. Interactively write these ideas on a chart, using bullets or another graphic organizer. These ideas do not have to be written in complete sentences; key words or phrases may be used. Explain that writers often organize their thoughts in this manner before actually beginning to write a paragraph or other piece of text.

- Reread the ideas that have been interactively written. Discuss the concept of a topic sentence and negotiate an appropriate topic sentence for this paragraph, based on the ideas generated.

- Reread the topic sentence. Refer again to the brainstormed list of key ideas. Discuss ideas for writing sentences that support and expand upon the topic sentence. Negotiate and write the sentences in sequential order.

- Reread the text. Discuss the need for a concluding sentence. Help the students to negotiate an appropriate conclusion that summarizes the key points of the paragraph.

Extensions

- Post the completed paragraph in the classroom. Label the topic sentence, supporting sentences, and concluding sentence. Use this as a reference when writing other paragraphs.

- Use interactive writing to create additional paragraphs about other content areas.

- Provide opportunities for the students to write paragraphs during independent writing or literacy centers.

Additional Resources

Carle, E. *The Grouchy Ladybug.* HarperCollins Children's Books, 1986. ISBN 0064434508

Dunbar, J. *Tick-Tock.* Lerner Publishing Group, 1998. ISBN 1575052512

Hopkins, L.B. *It's About Time!* Simon & Schuster Children's Publishing, 1993. ISBN 0671785125

Hutchins, P. *Clocks and More Clocks.* Simon & Schuster Children's Publishing, 1970. ISBN 0689717695

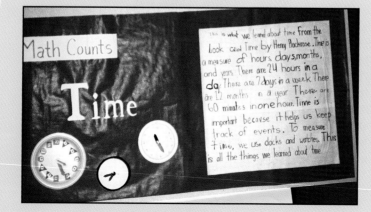

Here is a paragraph that summarizes what this third grade class knows about time.

Activity 53
Writing Process
Paragraph Development

Goal
Students will learn to organize sentences into paragraphs.

Areas of Study
Language Arts, Science

Interactive Writing Type
Negotiation

Resources
Nonfiction texts about the human body
Variety of media about the human body
Familiar shared reading pieces that are organized into
   paragraphs

Lessons

- During a unit of study about the human body, engage the students in numerous activities to build concept knowledge. Initiate discussions through the use of a variety of media, including read aloud books, films, posters, and slides.

- Using familiar shared reading pieces, focus the students' attention on the construction of a paragraph. Examine several familiar shared readings to see how authors present a main idea and use additional facts to support a topic statement. Locate topic sentences and describe their role in the paragraph.

- Introduce the students to the idea of brainstorming as a way to organize thoughts before writing. Help them to interactively write brainstorming charts, using knowledge gained in the current unit of study. During brainstorming, identify the main idea and supporting details.

- Use brainstorming charts to structure the interactive writing of paragraphs about parts of the human body.

- Refer to brainstorming charts as a resource frequently throughout the writing of paragraphs, and encourage the students to do the same when they are writing independently.

Extensions

- Create a literacy center that allows the students to practice writing paragraphs. Provide copies of the interactively written brainstorming charts. The students will write paragraphs, using the brainstorming charts as a guide.

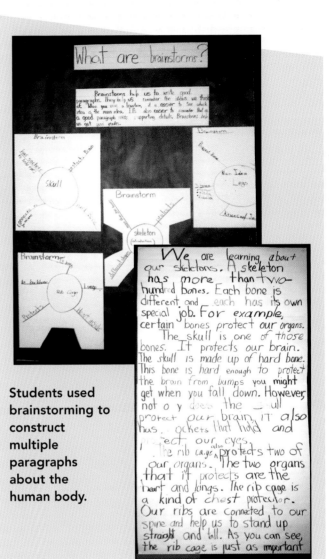

Students used brainstorming to construct multiple paragraphs about the human body.

- Encourage the students to research their own topics of interest and use the brainstorming strategy as a way to organize thoughts for writing paragraphs.

- Have the students use the brainstorming lists to write their own pieces about the human body.

Additional Resources
Arnold, T. *Parts.* Dial Books For Young Readers, 1997. ISBN 0803720408

Barnes, K., and Weston, S. *How It Works: The Human Body.* Barnes & Nobles Books, ISBN 0760704287

Cole, J., and Deger, B. *The Magic School Bus Inside the Human Body.* Scholastic, Inc., 1990. ISBN 0590414275

Activity 54
Written Language Conventions
Proofreading and Editing

Goal
Students will reread their writing and edit appropriately.

Areas of Study
Language Arts, Mathematics

Interactive Writing Type
Negotiation

Resources
A variety of mathematics books demonstrating the concept of multiplication

Lessons
- Read aloud a variety of books illustrating the concept of multiplication during a mathematics study introducing multiplication.

- Provide many hands-on investigations about multiplication in small groups, giving the students opportunities to discuss and understand the concept.

- Follow up small group investigations with whole group discussion to establish common agreements and understandings.

- Negotiate and write understandings about multiplication. During negotiation, emphasize that a numerical sentence must accompany the text to illustrate the meaning.

- Reread each sentence, proofreading for clearness and accuracy, editing as necessary.

- Demonstrate the use of caret marks for adding words when proofreading and editing.

Extensions
- Create a literacy center that gives students opportunities to write their own multiplication problems. Make these into a class book.

- Interactively create a class checklist for editing purposes.

This class discussed, wrote, reread, and edited their interactive piece about multiplication.

Additional Resources
Anno, M., and Anno, M. *Anno's Mysterious Multiplying Jar.* Putnam Publishing Group, 1983. ISBN 0399209514

Appelt, K. *Bats on Parade.* William Morrow & Co., 1999. ISBN 0688156657

Neuschwander, C., and Burns, M. *Amanda's Amazing Dream: A Mathematical Story.* Scholastic, Inc., 1998. ISBN 0590300121

Petty, K., and Maizels, J. *The Amazing Pop-Up Multiplication Book.* Dutton Children's Books, 1998. ISBN 0525459987

Attention and enthusiasm run high in interactive writing.

in•ter•ac•tive ed•it•ing

\in-te-ràk-tiv èd-it-in\

n. **1:** A teaching method in which children and teacher work together to edit familiar, error-free text. The reciprocity of reading and writing is a key feature of interactive editing. *n.* **2:** A powerful way to support literacy learning in children.

5. About Interactive Editing

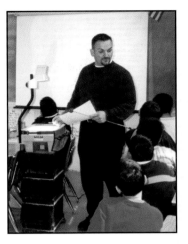

Interactive editing is a method of teaching effective writing in which teacher and students work together to edit correct text (what is called error-free text) that has been previously read (familiar) and not text that might have errors (such as their own writing). Editing from known material that is accurate provides an opportunity for students to understand how good writing is constructed in form, style, vocabulary, and other key elements, and how these understandings can be used or replicated in their own writing.

Interactive editing is also an effective way for teachers to model the thinking process that accompanies writing. Teachers can make a variety of teaching points in areas as diverse as grammar, phonics, spelling patterns, content, and the effective expression of ideas. It serves as a "think aloud" in which the construction of the text is explained, studied, and used as a model.

Interactive editing is a collaborative process. The teacher models the task the first time, shares the task the second time, and provides opportunities for independent practice. One key principle is that the strategies should be taught on accessible material at the students' independent level. Students work on more difficult text when they become more proficient and when the editing process is familiar. Too often, teaching a new strategy or skill is directed to new, difficult material.

Interactive editing is:

A strategy used to teach writing to both proficient and struggling readers.

Writing instruction in both form and content.

A model for writing from any content area.

Using the reading of text as a model to cooperatively write new products.

A strategy that supports comprehension through discussion.

A way to teach students different writing types and styles.

Introducing interactive editing with easy or very familiar content will make it a more successful way to teach and learn the writing process. In this way, material with increasingly greater challenges can be used with a high probability of success.

Interactive editing is not limited to any one type of writing. It helps students work with many genres and manipulate them in a way that helps them learn to write with better organization, using a wide variety of formats. Interactive editing is not intended to be used with all materials, nor is it intended to be a complete writing curriculum. It is a way to balance student work on shorter, informational writing with the personal response writing done in most classrooms.

Their Skin

An elephant's skin is wrinkled. The skin is almost one inch thick. It will burn if it is exposed to the sun for a long time. That is why elephants spend much of the day in the shade.

Elephants need to keep their skin in good condition. They bathe in water and spray the water over their backs with their trunks. They spray mud over themselves to make a mudpack. After they bathe, they throw dust over themselves. The mud and dust protects their skin from the hot sun. The mud and dust also protects them from biting insects and **parasites**, which are little animals that live and feed on their skin.

The only hairs on an adult elephant's skin are a few **bristles** around the trunk and two hard, thick patches of hair at the tip of the tail.

5

6. Getting Started

Example 1
Developing a List of Key Content Words

In Example 1, students are asked to identify words in the passage that are not critical to the meaning of the sentence or passage and can be eliminated. This approach may be more accessible for struggling readers and is a good first experience in determining important content vocabulary.

Step 1

Choose a short, high interest passage.

Copy the passage you are going to use onto an overhead transparency, either directly from the book or retyped in the same layout, and give a hard copy to each student.

Encourage the students to discuss the reading.

Step 2

Tell the students that the objective of this activity is to remove all of the unnecessary words so that only the key content words are left.

Step 3

Model crossing out the words that the students select as unnecessary on the overhead transparency.

Discuss the reasons that some words are important and other words are not important.

Here is an example of what students might develop.

Step 4
Independent work

Ask the students to copy the remaining words on a sheet of paper and construct sentences using the key content words.

Walk the room to observe and support the students' independent work.

Their Skin

An elephant's skin is wrinkled. ~~The skin is almost one~~ inch thick. ~~It will~~ burn ~~if it is exposed to the~~ sun ~~for a long time. That is why elephants spend much of the~~ day ~~in the~~ shade. ~~Elephants need to~~ keep ~~their~~ skin ~~in~~ good condition. ~~They~~ bathe ~~in~~ water ~~and~~ spray ~~the water over their backs with their trunks. They spray~~ mud ~~over themselves to make a~~ mudpack. ~~After they bathe, they throw~~ dust ~~over themselves. The mud and dust~~ protects ~~their skin from the hot sun. The mud and dust also protects them from biting~~ insects ~~and~~ parasites, ~~which are little animals that~~ live ~~and~~ feed ~~on their skin.~~

~~The only~~ hairs ~~on an adult elephant's skin are a few~~ bristles ~~around the~~ trunk, ~~and two hard, thick~~ patches ~~of hair at the tip of the~~ tail.

Step 5

Ask the students to share their work.

Work together as a class to develop consensus sentences.

Record this work on an overhead transparency.

Note: The value in this form of interactive editing is the teacher-led discussion about which words are critical to retain the message of the author. The end product will be different from the example, and the teaching points will vary, based on the needs of the students and the points that emerge during the discussion.

Example 2
Paraphrasing

Step 1

Copy the passage you are going to use onto a transparency, either directly from the book or retyped in the same layout, and give a hard copy to each student. For our example, we are going to use this passage from *Fish*.

Read the passage and ask the students to follow along on their copies.

Step 2

Choose a short, high interest passage and read it aloud.

Fish are animals that live in the water. All fish have fins.
Fins help fish swim. Fish have gills for breathing in the water.

Ask the students to read the passage together.

Step 3

Model how to go through the text and look at the ideas or units of thought and meaning. Chunk the text into units by circling the sections of text.

Discuss your reasons for choosing the key content words.

Use a blank overhead to list the first idea, unit of thought, or message in the passage. List: *fish, water, fins, gills, breathing.*

Instruct the students to turn over their copy of the reading and write the five words on the back.

fish
water
fins
gills
breathing

Instruct the students to turn over their copy of the reading and write the five words on the back.

Step 4

Say to the students: "I am going to reconstruct this as the first sentence in my rewrite. The goal is to develop a one-sentence paraphrase, using these five key content words."

One possible construction:
Fish use their fins to swim and their gills for breathing in water.

Text by Stanley L. Swartz   Photography by Robert Yin

Fish

Fish are animals that live in the water. All fish have fins. Fins help fish swim. Fish have gills for breathing in the water.

Fish swim in groups called schools. Schools are made up of many of the same kind of fish swimming together. Fish spend a lot of time swimming in schools. One school had more than three billion fish.

Fish come in many shapes. Some fish are big and some are small. Some fish have many colors. The colors help protect them.

Many fish live on coral reefs. There is plenty of food on these reefs. Fish eat plants and other fish. They swim and hide in the coral.

Step 5

Repeat this same process on paragraph two. Ask the students to read the passage aloud.

Fish swim in groups called schools. Schools are made up of many of the same kind of fish swimming together. Fish spend a lot of time swimming in schools. One school had more than three billion fish.

Step 6

Ask the students: "In the very first line of text, what would be the one word that carried the most meaning in the passage?"

Discuss the reasons and thinking behind their various choices. Use a transparency pen and circle the word they choose on the transparency. Then go to the next line and do the same.

Fish swim in groups called (schools.) Schools are made up of many of the same (kind) of fish (swimming) together. Fish spend a lot of time swimming in schools. One school had more than three (billion) fish.

Step 7

Instruct the students to list the key concept words on the back of their copy. Work together to develop a paraphrase of this passage. Write the attempts and corrections on a blank overhead.

Example: *Schools can be more than a billion fish of the same kind swimming together.*

This step should be repeated on other passages until the students demonstrate a good understanding of the process.

Step 8
Independent practice

Ask the students to follow the same procedures on the next passage and create a paraphrase of their own. Walk the classroom to observe and guide individual efforts.

Step 9

Ask the students to select one or two important words from each paraphrase and write a summary statement for the entire reading.

Example:

Passage 1 selection: *fins, gills*
Passage 2 selection: *schools*
Passage 3 selection: *shapes, colors*
Passage 4 selection: *coral reefs, food*

Example of Summary Statement:

Schools of fish of many shapes and colors use their gills and fins to swim around coral reefs and find their food.

Questions should include:
Does this passage have the same meaning as the original?
Have we improved the passage with our work?
Are there other changes we might make to improve our work?

All of this work and the successive attempts should be recorded on the overhead transparency. Consider it a work in progress and make the point that the need for corrections is part of the process.

Step 10

Ask the students to reconstruct this passage, using the summary statement as the first sentence, paraphrase 1 as the second sentence, paraphrase 2 as the third sentence, paraphrase 3 as the fourth sentence, and paraphrase 4 as the last sentence. Read this new passage aloud and discuss the impact of their work.

Step 11

Tell the students that the final task of this activity is to write a new concluding sentence.

Revise the summary statement as a concluding sentence by restating it or reversing the subject and the predicate. Use the overhead project as a worksheet and record attempts and edits.

Example:

Fish with many colors and shapes find their food around coral reefs and swim in schools using their fins and gills.

Note: Remember that the discussions that accompany this work are as valuable as the final product. Discussions should be as extensive as possible and used to focus on the writing process and how we make meaning of the message that the author of the passage is trying to send. Teaching points will vary according to the needs of the students and the issues that are raised in the discussions.

Example 3
Rewriting as a Shortened Piece (Telegram)

Step 1

Tell the students that the objective of this activity is to rewrite a text retaining only the critical information, using the form of a telegram.

Today's weather forecast is for unseasonably warm temperatures that are expected to reach into the middle to upper 70s Fahrenheit, 20s Centigrade, by mid day.

TELEGRAM

Today's weather is warm.

Note: Because many students are unfamiliar with telegrams, give them a brief history. However, most students will understand the objective in monetary terms.

Tell the students that people who send telegrams are charged by the number of words used; more words, greater cost. Our job is to send the message for as little money as possible. The concept of a short e-mail message could also be used.

There is one restriction in this form of interactive editing. The message must consist of sentences (at least a subject and a verb). Model this procedure by putting this sentence on the overhead transparency and editing it to a telegram. Circle the key content words.

Step 2

Read the passage below to the students from a full copy of text on the overhead transparency.

Step 3

Teacher and students should work on the example together. Work through the text collaboratively, circling the key content words. Remind them that sentence structure must be retained.

Students frequently ask questions about whether they can change the order of words, add a verb, or change verb tense. This kind of flexible thinking should be encouraged, as long as the objective of creating concise sentences is not lost.

Step 4

Review the end product together. Use this debriefing opportunity to remind the students of the process they went through and the value of this kind of analysis.

The end product might look like this:

> Spokesmen for the Centers for Disease Control (CDC), an official agency of the United States Government, reported today in a telephone interview that an outbreak of measles is considered to be at the level of an epidemic in young children aged three to seven. Speaking from their main office in Atlanta, Georgia, the spokesmen indicated that their remarks would also be issued as a national news bulletin to be released this afternoon. The CDC has discovered new information that found some of the measles vaccinations supply provided to doctors and hospitals in the last ten years were not effective. Parents of children in this age group will be advised to check with their physicians to determine if their child received any of the measles vaccination from this supply.

T E L E G R A M

Measles is an epidemic in young children. Bulletin to be released. Vaccinations were not effective. Parents advised to check with physician.

Spokesmen for the Centers for Disease Control (CDC), an official agency of the United States Government, reported today in a telephone interview that an outbreak of measles is considered to be at the level of an epidemic in young children aged three to seven. Speaking from their main office in Atlanta, Georgia, the spokesmen indicated that their remarks would also be issued as a national news bulletin to be released this afternoon. The CDC has discovered new information that found some of the measles vaccinations supply provided to doctors and hospitals in the last ten years were not effective. Parents of children in this age group will be advised to check with their physicians to determine if their child received any of the measles vaccination from this supply.

Step 5

Independent practice

Provide the students with a hard copy of a selection from the newspaper or a magazine and ask them to edit it to a telegram.

Divide the class into small groups. Select your five lowest children and work directly with them on this task. Allow other groups to work independently.

Step 6

Ask the students to share their work. Work through the independent practice example as a group on the overhead.

Develop a consensus telegram, combining the students' independent work.

Note: As with the other interactive editing procedures, the discussions that accompany this work present many and varied teaching opportunities. Follow the lead of student comments, but don't hesitate to guide the discussion to important teaching points.

Postscript

These are just three examples of procedures to use in interactive editing. As teachers gain more experience with this method, ways to innovate on the procedure and modify it for their own use will become apparent.

7. Interactive Editing Procedures

Before the Editing

Classroom Setup

Interactive editing requires no special classroom setup. Seating arrangements can vary, but it is important that all children are able to see the overhead projector or chart paper and see and hear the teacher. Classroom setup considerations might also include grouping needs for follow-up activities or extensions, such as placing low children in one group for direct teacher assistance.

Setting the Instructional Purpose

Interactive editing is an opportunity for teachers to model writing with a wide variety of instructional purposes. Teachers share their thinking and demonstrate how to work with text and understand the writing process in both form and content. It is appropriate for all types of text, but particularly supports learning in nonfiction materials. The specific purposes selected for each lesson are often based on teacher observations during independent writing or other independent student work.

While personal response to literature is an important aspect of the writing process, another important aspect of writing in the classroom is informational writing. In real-life experiences, people write notes, e-mails, phone messages, memos, recipes, business letters, grocery lists, and many other types of expository writing. Interactive editing is an effective method to work on these kinds of writing purposes. It cannot be assumed that the writing skills needed to write essays, reports, short stories, and poems will automatically transfer to the other types of writing and develop by themselves without instruction. The standardized tests used most often in grades two and higher test reading comprehension through selections that are informational and based on science and social studies, with selections that include maps, graphs, charts, and recipes. Practice with these forms of writing with an emphasis on the reciprocity of reading and writing is a key purpose of interactive editing.

> ## What Happens Before the Interactive Editing
>
> Teacher chooses a text, based on instructional needs.
>
> Teacher and students read text together.
>
> Plan and discuss the editing goal.
>
> Choose the type of interactive editing.
>
> Prepare overhead and individual copies of text.

Beginning Points for Interactive Editing

There are many ways to start an interactive editing lesson. Teachers select materials, based on content considerations and possible teaching points. Take time to carefully choose text in the content area you are responsible for teaching or something that supports other ongoing work in the classroom. Keep in mind that nonfiction is emphasized, though a variety of texts can be used:

- nonfiction paragraphs from textbooks
- science, social studies, health, mathematics
- paragraphs from newspapers and periodicals
- songs and poems
- fiction, from both school and personal sources
- previous read aloud books excerpts and shared readings

Types of Interactive Editing

Determining and Listing Key Content Words

In this type of interactive editing students are asked to locate the key content words in the selected text. This is the most basic form of interactive editing; it helps students to begin analyzing text and locating words or phrases that are most important in conveying content and the message. Lists of these words or phrases can be used for various group projects as well as independent writing. The important aspect is the process of working through the text as a group and the discussion that takes place during the process.

Example of Listing Key Content Words:
Students are asked to circle and list the key content words on the back of their copy of the text while the teacher circles the words on the overhead copy.

Jellyfish
**From *Marine Life for Young Readers*
published by Dominie Press**

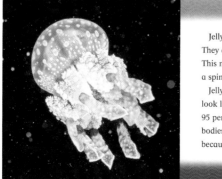

Jellyfish are not really fish at all. They are actually invertebrates. This means they do not have a spine, or backbone.

Jellyfish get their name because they look like jelly. They are made up of 95 percent water. Most jellyfish have bodies you can see through because they are clear.

Jellyfish are (not) really (fish) at all. They are actually (invertebrates.) This means they do not have a spine, or backbone.

Jellyfish get their name because they look like jelly. They are made up of (95 percent) (water.) Most jellyfish have bodies you can see through because they are (clear.)

Students might develop the following list of key content words:
Paragraph 1: *not, fish, invertebrates*
Paragraph 2: *95 percent, water, clear*

After the development of this list as a whole group activity, the students can be grouped to use this list in various writing tasks, or they might be asked to use them in an independent writing activity.

Paraphrasing

In the paraphrasing type of interactive editing, students are asked to select key content words and use them to restate the sentence, paragraph, or idea. They use paraphrasing as a way to edit text to clarify the meaning, make it shorter, or use their own words while preserving the meaning of the original text.

Example of Paraphrasing:
The students circle the key content words on their copy while the teacher marks the overhead copy.

Students might select the following key content words:
Paragraph 1: *eels, snakes, coral reefs*
Paragraph 2: *sharp teeth, eat, fish, gills, breathe*

And they might develop the following paraphrases:
Paragraph 1: *Eels look like snakes and live around coral reefs.*
Paragraph 2: *They have sharp teeth to eat fish and use gills to breathe.*

Summarizing

As a last step, students combine the two paraphrases into a summary statement.
Example: *Eels look like snakes and eat fish with their sharp teeth.*

Eels
From ***Marine Life for Young Readers***
published by Dominie Press

Eels are long fish that look like snakes. They live in oceans all over the world. Many eels live around coral reefs.

Eels have strong, sharp teeth. They eat other fish. Eels use their gills to breathe under water.

(Eels) are long fish that look like (snakes.) They live in oceans all over the world. Many eels live around (coral reefs.) Eels have strong, (sharp teeth.) They (eat) other (fish.) Eels use their (gills) to (breathe) under water.

Editing to a Shortened Piece

Another way to develop an understanding of important content in text is to reverse the process and ask the students to locate words that are not critical to the content or message of the text. This is sometimes an easier starting point when they have more difficulty with reading a selection or have little background knowledge about a topic. When using this approach to edit to a telegram, students are usually asked to use a sentence form. Other shortened pieces might use phrases or sentence fragments similar to some messages that are sent by e-mail or memorandum. Students are usually motivated in this task when it is framed as an economy of words that converts to a lower cost for sending the message.

Example of Editing to a Telegram:

Students are instructed to cross out words on their copy. The teacher does the same on the overhead copy, leaving only the important words.

This morning ~~at approximately 2 a.m., Pacific Standard Time, an~~ earthquake struck ~~the City of~~ Los Angeles, ~~California and surrounding cities along the coast of the Pacific Ocean. The area is believed to have suffered~~ severe damage ~~to both housing and commercial~~ buildings ~~as well as streets and bridges. There has been no report of~~ injuries ~~or possible fatalities but government~~ officials ~~are cautiously~~ optimistic.

> ### T E L E G R A M
>
> Earthquake struck Los Angeles
> this morning. Buildings
> severely damaged. Officials
> optimistic about injuries.

Students are given the flexibility to change word order, word form, and even to add a word. However, the meaning of the original message must be maintained.

Changing Writing Categories

Interactive editing can also take the form of helping students understand various writing purposes and formats by using the process to change the category of the original text.

Text might be changed from:

- narrative to poetry
- expository to. narrative
- expository to test-taking questions
- narrative to reader's theater

Example of Changing Writing Categories:

Students are given the task of developing a poem from the selected text. All ideas and work are put on the overhead transparency by the teacher. The students are also instructed to list their ideas on their copy of the text.

The editing task for this selection can be handled in various ways. One way is for the students to rewrite the narrative text to a poem. Show them the traditional children's nursery rhyme as an example and ask them to write a poem of their own.

Two young college students were asked by their professor to pick up supplies for their chemistry class. One of the students, Jack Jones, is a chemistry major, and the other student, Jill Jacobs, is taking the course as an elective. The company that supplies colleges with chemicals is located in the foothills of the San Bernardino Mountains. Jack agreed to use his car and Jill agreed to bring the necessary containers for the supplies. During the trip, Jack's car broke down and they had to walk the last block to the supply company. Only H2O was available on their supply list, and Jack filled the round container brought by Jill. As they left the store, both Jack and Jill slipped and fell, and Jack hurt his head.

Jack and Jill went up the hill
to fetch a pail of water.
Jack fell down and broke his crown
and Jill came tumbling after.

Example:
Jack and Jill were college students
and they might have not been prudent.
On an errand for a friend
their car broke down around the bend.
Water spilled is water lost.
They both fell down at what a cost.

Another Example of Changing Writing Category:
Students are asked to take the expository selection and make a list of the sequence of the steps or events involved. These steps then might be made into a poem or a dialogue. The process of changing text from one category to another helps students think about key words and the meaning of the text. They can also learn to be flexible and use the same ideas in more than one writing category.

The text is converted to a list of steps and then rewritten.

The word *step* and the number are inserted into the original text. The students are then asked to edit their work and remove extraneous details.

New text is written for the new steps.

Step 1 Two young college students were asked by their professor to pick up supplies for their chemistry class. One of the students, Jack Jones, is a chemistry major, and the other student, Jill Jacobs, is taking the course as an elective. Step 2 The company that supplies colleges with chemicals is located in the foothills of the San Bernardino Mountains. Jack agreed to use his car and Jill agreed to bring the necessary containers for the supplies. Step 3 During the trip, Jack's car broke down and they had to walk the last block to the supply company. Only H$_2$0 was available on their supply list, and Jack filled the round container brought by Jill. Step 4 As they left the store, both Jack and Jill slipped and fell, and Jack hurt his head.

> Step 1
> Two young college students were asked by their professor to pick up supplies for their chemistry class–Jack Jones and Jill Jacobs
> Step 2
> The company is located in the San Bernardino Mountains. Jack agreed to use his car and Jill agreed to bring the containers.
> Step 3
> Jack's car broke down and they had to walk the last block. Only H2O was available and Jack filled the round container brought by Jill.
> Step 4
> As they left, both slipped and fell and Jack hurt his head.

Choosing the Text
The text should be carefully chosen from both nonfiction and fiction texts. The selection might come from a read aloud book, or the shared reading of a paragraph, poem, or chart. Other choices might be made from social studies, science, math, and health textbooks or a newspaper or magazine article.

The selected text is usually short (up to 100 words) and at the instructional level where children can work without frustration while still learning in the selection. It is helpful for the students to have some prior knowledge of the subject, though this can also be handled to a great extent in the discussion that accompanies the shared reading. Not enough can be said about the importance of selecting something that the students are likely to find interesting and therefore more likely to maintain their interest during the editing process. Texts for first efforts should be relatively simple, nonfiction passages that can be reread fairly easily by the students. Because the process of editing is the primary goal, materials that are controversial and provoke strong opinions will slow the process. With a group-edited product as the goal, rather than some type of personal response, literature stories or complicated, technical text should be used only after the children are very familiar with the goals of editing. Once the process and strategies are understood, all forms of fiction and nonfiction text should be used.

> ## Things to Consider When Choosing Text to Edit
>
> *Appropriate readability (independent or easy instructional level)*
>
> *Relatively short passage that conveys a complete idea*
>
> *Some prior knowledge of the subject*
>
> *Relevant tie to standards*
>
> *Potential for student interest and engagement*

Materials Needed for Interactive Editing

Interactive editing requires few specific materials. Most teachers prefer the use of an overhead projector where they can display a copy of the text and show the work in progress. An alternative would be the use of chart paper or a large piece of butcher paper where the work can also be shown with the use of markers. Students receive a hard copy of the selection with both of these options. They are asked to attend to the whole class work and, with teacher direction, complete the work on their individual copy. Teachers who have developed word walls in their classrooms will find them useful during interactive editing. Consider the addition of word families on the word wall if they have not already been included.

> ## Materials Needed
>
> *one copy of the text on a transparency*
>
> *chart or butcher paper as an alternative*
>
> *hard copy for each student*
>
> *overhead, markers, and screen*
>
> *word wall of high frequency words and word families*
>
> *Optional materials*
>
> *content word walls*
>
> *previous class writings*
>
> *informational charts*

During the Editing

Read the selection of text and discuss with the students whether it makes sense to them. Do they understand the message of the author? Can they restate the message in their own words? The teacher should clarify unknown words, phrases, ideas, and concepts and relate the text to something the students know or something studied in a content area. Student questions and comments should be encouraged throughout this process. The desired end result of this discussion is a basic comprehension of the text.

The teacher and students should select the type of interactive editing product they want to develop. Choices might be the development of paraphrases or

What Happens During the Interactive Editing

Teacher and/or students read the text.

Discuss the meaning of the text.

Model and think aloud the editing procedure.

Edit the text and discuss the work in progress.

Teacher shows the work on the overhead.

Students record work on their copy.

modifying the text to a telegram form. The teacher should model and think aloud the process of editing. Teachers can guide the process to teaching points identified before the reading as well as those that come up during the work in progress.

Using a Work Sheet

As the teacher works on the overhead, students work on their individual copies. All work can be marked on the copy or on the back, or special work sheets might be used. Below are three examples of work sheets that might help students organize their thoughts and ideas.

Word Bank	Error-Free Text Is Written Here
Summary Statement(s):	

Word Bank	Paraphrase Statement
Word Bank	**Paraphrase Statement**
Word Bank	**Paraphrase Statement**

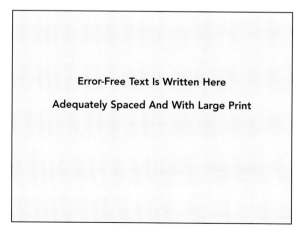

Error-Free Text Is Written Here

Adequately Spaced And With Large Print

Transition from Teacher to Student Responsibility

Over time the teacher can gradually release much of the editing responsibility to the students. As students select words that they consider important words, they should be asked to explain their choices. The teacher models how to use these important words to create a paraphrase or a summary statement. This is when a word wall might be useful. It is helpful for students to think about categories of words and how most text is constructed. The summary sentence and the paraphrases can easily be made into a paragraph, with the summary becoming the main idea and the paraphrases becoming the detail sentences. This process helps model for the students how to go from key words to note cards or list to paragraph and report writing.

At first this process is done one idea at a time. The teacher models it, then the teacher and students do the next one together, a group of students might do another one, and eventually this support helps students to complete the task on their own. The teacher may have to model the process several times before the students understand how to begin.

Transition from Interactive Editing to Other Writing Needs

It is important not to assume that students will make the connection between the writing strategies that are taught in interactive editing and the writing of essays and reports. The purpose of the writing and how what you learn can be used in other ways should always be clear. The goal of the teacher is to teach for transfer and application of strategies to other tasks.

The writing strategy being used:
- Shows how to determine key vocabulary in all subjects.
- Teaches how to rewrite information that has been read and learned into an essay or report.
- Helps students become better writers in class and in real life.
- Makes writing easier and manageable.

> ## Most writing contains:
>
> 67-70% high frequency words (*is*, *in*, *the*)
> 18% content words (*earthquake*)
> 12-14% modifiers or qualifiers (*quietly*)

> ## Questions to Ask in Interactive Editing
>
> *Is my modeling direct and explicit?*
>
> *Do I use observations to develop lessons?*
>
> *Is the amount of time for lessons appropriate?*
>
> *Can I see students becoming more independent?*
>
> *Do I revisit the process frequently?*

Teaching Points

Interactive editing uses the discussion between the teacher and the students as the primary method to make teaching points. Selection of text and the discussion guides specific teaching points selected by the teacher. The collaboration is a way to help students think about what is needed to change the text and does not mean that the teacher should relinquish the role as facilitator. Direct, explicit instruction is an essential part of interactive editing.

Because interactive editing is effective with more proficient readers and writers, the teaching points are shifted to higher levels. The reality in many classrooms, however, is a variety of levels of ability, ranging from students who are struggling with basic concepts to children who have control of much of the writing process. Interactive editing provides flexibility for teachers to make both basic and advanced teaching points during the same lesson.

Alphabetic Principle

Most of the information in alphabetic principle is the focus of work with beginning readers. Letter recognition and formation are usually mastered, but higher functioning students still need work in handwriting. Letter-name correspondence is an unlikely focus, but work on letter-sound correspondence might need reinforcement. Alphabetic order can become a task of higher complexity and is used in various ways in interactive editing lessons.

Alphabetic Principle
• Letter formation and handwriting
• Letter-sound correspondence
• Alphabetic order

Concepts about Print

Early concepts about print are under the control of more proficient readers and writers. Directionality, one-to-one matching, and return sweep are concepts that should require little instruction. Spacing applied to indentation, paragraph form, charts, and text layout are useful teaching points. Word, sentence, and story order can also be part of the lesson. Nonfiction texts used by many of these students have a very complicated layout. The typical science text has graphs, charts, boxes of text, and highlighted words and phrases, all on one page. Understanding how to process and use this text is important support for later content learning.

Concepts about Print
• Spacing, indentation, paragraph form, charts, and text layout
• Concept of first and last part of word, sentence, and story
• Reading the punctuation

Phonemic Awareness and Phonics

Many of our struggling readers and writers and English language learners will need support in many of the skills used in phonemic awareness and phonics. The Writing Checklist (see Page 127) provides a way to determine what skill development a student might need. It is important not to overemphasize this area when students have the skills under their control. Only make the necessary teaching points and allow the students the opportunity to use what they already know.

Phonemic Awareness and Phonics
Hearing sounds in words
Inflectional endings
Rhyming
Syllabication
Compound words
Onset and rime
Segmentation
Chunking and blending
Root words
Sounds in sequence
Analogies
High frequency words
Spelling patterns
Consonants, blends, short and long vowels, digraphs, diphthongs
Alliteration
Suffixes, prefixes

Written Language Skills
Interactive editing is an opportunity to model written language skills in an ongoing writing activity instead of using practice formats that are isolated, such as word sheets. Though all of the skills will not come up in a single lesson, as interactive editing is used over time, many can be included, based on teacher observation and assessment of student need.

Written Language Skills
Punctuation and capitalization
Spelling and word analysis
Sentence structure
Grammar
Similes and metaphors
Homophones, antonyms, and synonyms
Parts of speech
Word usage
Irregular words
Onomatopoeia
Contractions

Writing Process
Similar to the opportunities provided to work on written language conventions, interactive editing is a way to model how ideas are developed and how we organize the text that we want to write. The discussions that accompany making word choices and selecting genre are then followed up in group activities and independent writing.

Writing Process

Idea development

Text organization

Proofreading and editing

Outlining

Vocabulary and word choice

Concept development

Characters, setting, and plot

Writing categories

Paragraph development

What Happens after the Interactive Editing

Reread the edited work.

Discuss the impact of the work.

Students work in small groups.

Extend the writing into other activities.

Apply learning to independent writing.

After the Editing

Teachers can select various ways to reinforce the concepts that have been worked on during the editing process. The work should be reread aloud by the teacher and the students. The discussion should focus on what work was completed and what the impact of that work is on the original text. Did it change the meaning? Did we improve the text?

Group work can be another way to continue the activity. Groups might be given a specific assignment, like taking the edited text and changing the genre. A group might also complete the work that was initiated in the whole-class activity. This gives the teacher an opportunity to make different teaching points to different students.

Uses for Completed Interactive Editing

The writing products of interactive editing are artifacts that can be used by students to support other writing lessons. Posting the end product developed by the whole class reminds the students of how the product was developed. This also provides support for their independent writing and acts like a writing prompt during future lessons. Specific skills that have been taught can be highlighted and posted and referred to during other lessons, or the attention of an individual student might be directed to the work. Similarly, work on content area topics can be supported by the access and availability of the class writing samples.

A lesson portfolio of work is recommended for each student to use as samples of specific types of writing. Students have available for their use a correct text that they helped develop. These examples are useful models and can be transferred to their independent writing.

Group Activities

When the teacher and the students become familiar with the interactive editing process, the same skills can be taken to increasingly challenging texts. As an example, if a graphic organizer is being used during interactive editing, the teacher might make an independent writing assignment in which students try to transfer this organizer to new reading and content selections. This would be a good time to group low students with a similar need to provide direct instruction before the whole class moves forward in a whole-group activity.

Rather than transitioning from whole-class activities to independent work and then back to whole class, grouping of students can be an effective way to provide individual support.

Grouping might be both homogeneous and heterogeneous at the same time, with the teacher free to move among groups and make specific teaching points. Small-group work is an opportunity for students to transfer and apply what they have learned in the whole-class activity, but with some support. Application of learning in independent work is the goal, but this step can be supported through the interaction of others in the group.

Extensions

The multiple types of writing products developed through interactive editing provide a unique opportunity for students to combine different types that they have written in the extension activities. These writing lessons and products do not stand alone but are meant to build and combine with other examples to create more complex writing. The understanding of multiple text types includes the ability to transfer and combine formats and produce new examples and ways to express information. Once they are proficient in the strategies, the students can rewrite their own original pieces this way, or peer edit final drafts of other students' work in the same manner. The flexibility learned as students combine formats is an essential part of becoming an independent writer.

Activity 59
Interactive Editing
Conventions

Goal
Students will identify and purposefully use a variety of punctuation symbols.

Areas of Study
Language Arts, Social Studies, Mathematics, Science

Resources
Shared reading from any content area
Highlighter tape
Magna Doodle, markers, poster paper, correction tape

Lessons
- As a class, read a shared reading from any content area.

- After the meaning is explored, identify, highlight, and discuss the purposes for punctuation used in the shared reading.

- Move and/or change the punctuation in the shared reading piece.

- Reread to note if meaning and fluency are affected by the change in punctuation.

- Provide discussion time for the students to share how their thinking about punctuation may have changed.

- As a class, decide how to record the information so it can be used for future reference.

- Interactively negotiate and record the information.

- Display the information for future student reference.

Extensions
- Students will keep individual journals of additional punctuation symbols and their purposes.

Additional Resources
Hope, D., and Anders, T. *Punctuation Pals.* Alpine Publishing, 2000. ISBN 1885624565

McKerns, D., and Motchkavitz, L. *The Kid's Guide to Good Grammar: What You Need to Know about Punctuation, Sentence Structure, Spelling and More.* Lowell House Juvenile, 1998. ISBN 1565656970

Terban, M. *Punctuation Power: Punctuation and How to Use It.* Scholastic, Inc., 2000. ISBN 0590386735

While studying simple machines, this class also identified and explored uses of punctuation, highlighted in red. To organize their thinking, the students constructed a table of definitions for various punctuation symbols.

Activity 60
Interactive Editing
Diaries: Formal and Informal

Goals
Students will identify purposes for writing diaries; and write diary entries, using formal and informal diary text structures.

Areas of Study
Language Arts, Social Studies, Mathematics, Science

Resources
Several shared readings of diaries, both formal and informal, representing various disciplines

Two shared readings of diary entries, describing the same account from different points of view

Lessons
- As a class, read and discuss the examples of various diary entries.

- Engage the students in discussions about the purposes for writing diaries. Also discuss the differences between formal and informal diary text structures, including personal and impersonal use of language.

- Read two shared readings of diary entries representing the same account from differing viewpoints. Discuss how perspective is a part of constructing meaning when reading text.

- As a class, change one of the diary entries to reflect another perspective, engaging the students in a discussion about what specific changes this will involve; for example, word choice, conventions, and text structure. This will require much discussion about the authors of the diary entries, as well as their writing styles.

Extensions
- Individually create diary entries using formal diary formats representing various disciplines such as explorer, social scientist, engineer, or writer.

- Create a time line representing events written about in given diary entries.

July 13, 1851

Dear Diary,
Today was a very difficult day for all of us. It started out with huge black rain clouds threatening to deliver a summer rain storm. Not far out of camp a wheel on the lead wagon broke. It was the skill and quick thinking of Mr. Johnson that narrowly averted a catastrophe. The way Mr. Johnson kept a tight, steady rein on the horses prevented them from panicking.
    I hope tomorrow is a much calmer day.
                    Sarah

July 13, 1851

Dear Diary,
    This day presented a number of obstacles that could have easily been avoided. I must admit I am quite distressed that it might be my own carelessness that caused a near tragedy on this day. I did not check the wheels on my wagon closely enough and I fear that oversight nearly cost me my worldly goods. I must not repeat this mistake.
                    Ned Johnson

This diary entry was interactively edited by a group of students.

Additional Resources
Denenberg, B. *The Journal of William Thomas Emerson, A Revolutionary War Patriot (Dear America Series)*. Scholastic, Inc., 1998. ISBN 0590313509

McKissack, P. *Nzingha: Warrior Queen of Matamba*. Scholastic, Inc., 2000. ISBN 0439112109

Moss, M. *Amelia's Notebook*. Pleasant Company Publications, 1999. ISBN 1562477846

Activity 61
Interactive Editing
Expository Text Structure

Goal
Students will understand the structure and organization of expository text. They will purposefully apply this knowledge in their independent writing.

Areas of Study
Language Arts, Social Studies, Mathematics, Science

Resources
Shared reading texts covering a specific idea, person, or event
Magna Doodle, markers, poster paper, correction tape

Lessons
- Using several read aloud and shared reading texts, explore a specific idea, person, or event.

- Lead the students into a discussion about the need and purposes for organizing information and schema in our thinking and on paper.

- As a class, decide upon which graphic organizer to use. Also decide upon the major topics and details to be recorded on the organizer.

- Using interactive writing, complete the graphic organizer while the students engage in discussions concerning both the purposes and strategies for organizing thoughts and written material.

- During following lessons, use the graphic organizer to construct a paragraph, again, providing opportunity for the students to discuss the purposes and strategies for writing the expository text.

- Label parts of the expository paragraph, including the topic sentence, supporting details, and concluding sentence.

- Display both the organizer and the paragraph in the classroom for future reference by the students.

Extensions
- In small groups write additional paragraphs, using the information on the class web. As a class, compile and organize the paragraphs into a complete document for future topic review and text structure reference.

Additional Resources
Giblin, J. *Thomas Jefferson (A Picture Book Biography)*. Scholastic, Inc., 1994. ISBN 0590448382

Giblin, J. *The Amazing Life of Benjamin Franklin*. Scholastic, Inc., 2000. ISBN 0590485342

Krensky, S. *Taking Flight: The Story of the Wright Brothers*. Simon & Schuster Children's, 2000. ISBN 0689812256

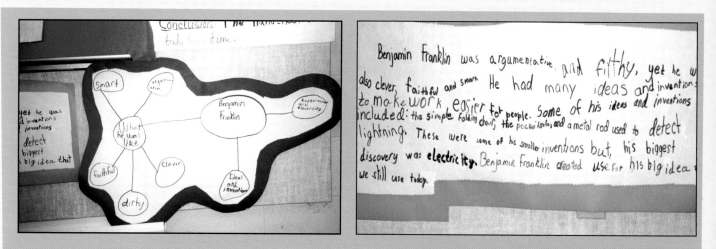

A class studying Benjamin Franklin wanted to use their knowledge while learning to organize ideas and write expository paragraphs.

Activity 62
Interactive Editing
Instructions

Goal
Students will read and write instructions with a critical eye.

Areas of Study
Language Arts, Social Studies, Mathematics, Science

Resources
Shared readings of examples of instructions in various formats
One shared reading of instructions in paragraph format
Magna Doodle, markers, poster paper, correction tape

Lessons

• As a class, read and discuss several examples of instructions.

• Engage the students in a discussion about various writing needs.

• Include discussions regarding layout of text, sequence of text, types of words used, conventions used, and why a certain text layout would be chosen in a given situation.

• Discuss the differences between verbal and written directions.

• Read a shared reading of instructions in a paragraph format.

• As a class, discuss ways to change text format and make the meaning more clear.

• Interactively negotiate and rewrite text into a sequential list format, discussing use of appropriate conventions as needed.

Extensions

• Change the text layout of directions in a sequential list into a paragraph format.

• Individually or in pairs, write directions for routines in the classroom and school. Compile these into a classroom resource for new students.

Additional Resource
Katzen, M. *Honest Pretzels: And 64 Other Amazing Recipes For Cooks Age 8 And Up.* Tricycle Press, 1999. ISBN 1883672880

...TO Mrs. Pollard's office

1. Go out the south door
2. Turn WEST (right)
3. Walk past the Library
4. Go through the double doors
5. Walk down the hall to the third door on the left
6. Go through the third door on the left
7. Go past the teacher's lounge
8. Turn right at the T (intersection)
9. Mrs. Pollard's office is the last door on the left

After reading a paragraph description of how to get to a teacher's office, this class rewrote the instructions into a sequential list format, making the instructions easier to follow. This activity also led into a study of maps, their purposes and construction.

Activity 63
Interactive Editing
Math Word Problems

Goal
Students will identify and use key words to solve math word problems.

Area of Study
Mathematics

Resources
Shared reading of math word problems
Magna Doodle, markers, poster paper, correction tape

Lessons
- Share read math story problems together. Concentrate on one operation.

- Discuss and solve them as a class, stressing the importance of listening for key words and signal words providing clues for solving the problem. If necessary, act out parts of the word problem to increase the meaning and conceptual development of the operation being studied.

- After the students are secure with addition word problems, as a class, use the shared reading to rewrite questions asking for different problem-solving tasks such as division or multiplication.

- Negotiate and interactively write the problem-solving question.

- When the writing is finished, reread the question to determine whether it makes sense. Highlight and search for key words that could serve as clues for solving the new word problem.

Extensions
- Individually or in pairs, write additional word problems. Compile them into a class book providing opportunities to apply problem-solving strategies.

- Interactively write steps and strategies for solving math word problems.

Additional Resources
Burns, M. *The Book of Think: Or How To Solve A Problem Twice Your Size.* Little, Brown & Company, 1976. ISBN 0316117439

Burns, M. *Spaghetti and Meatballs For All!: A Mathematical Story.* Scholastic, Inc., 1998. ISBN 0590944592

Scieszka, J. *Math Curse.* Viking Children's Books, 1995. ISBN 0670861944

Problem
$7 + 3 = 10$

Key Number Words
Seven
three

Key Function Words
How many
altogether

Sentences
Seven and three equals ten.
Seven plus three equals ten.
Seven and three makes ten.
Seven and three more makes ten.

There were seven cats playing by the tree. Then three dogs came to play too. How many animals were playing by the tree altogether?

Students identified key math function words in order to solve this story problem and others like it.

Activity 64
Interactive Editing
Persuasive Writing

Goal
Student will read with a critical eye to distinguish fact from opinion, and identify various perspectives and points of view.

Areas of Study
Language Arts, Social Studies, Mathematics, Science

Resources
Editorials on any topic representing opposing points of view
Markers, poster paper, correction tape

Lessons
• Share read opposing editorials.

• Discuss the meaning of the text. Emphasize the arrangement of text, the emotive words used, repetitions, and whether the arguments are written in past, present, or future tense.

• Discuss strategies for distinguishing fact from opinion.

• As a class, identify the main ideas represented, including strategies for critically identifying the main ideas, as well as the author's strategies for presenting his points of view.

• Engage the students in an oral argument defending an opposing view to one of the editorials.

• Discuss the differences between oral and written arguments.

• Interactively revise an editorial so that it represents an opposing viewpoint. Include discussions about word choice, repetition of ideas, conventions, and perspectives involved.

Extensions
• In pairs or small groups, write editorials about issues concerning the students. Also orally present their viewpoints. Provide opportunity for discussion contrasting the oral and written presentation of viewpoints.

• Individually or in pairs, summarize an editorial. Write a response regarding its practicality and validity, using strategies identified during whole-group discussions.

• Interactively write a list of strategies to use when reading editorials with a critical eye.

Editorial Page

In reading The News Enterprise article about XYZ Charter School declaring bankruptcy, I was struck by the fact that so many charter schools are being starved of funds and having to go under. The biggest problem as I see it is that the fox is in charge of the hen house. When you put a school in charge of a charter school, the district has a vested interest in seeing them fall.

Anywhere, USA had trouble keeping its five charter schools running until an independent board was put in place to oversee them and they now have over 300 charter schools. By withholding funds, the DEF School Board and the State of Everywhere are circumventing the will of the people who have demanded school reform and mandated charter schools. People need to stand up and demand that their will is carried out.

John Doe, Everywhere

ABC School Board accuses XYZ Charter School, XYZCS, a charter school under its jurisdiction, of not keeping accurate attendance records. Enter the XYZ auditors who found no errors in XYZCS.

If its own auditors found no errors, ABC School Board should admit its own error and stop making false accusations.

Jane Smith, Landville

The class worked from these editorials to interactively edit persuasive text.

Additional Resources
Dorris, M. *Morning Girl*. Hyperion Books for Children, 1992. ISBN 1562822845

Scieszka, J. *The True Story of the Three Little Pigs*. Penguin Putnam Books for Young Readers, 1996. ISBN 0140544518

Yolen, J. *Encounter*. Harcourt, Inc., 1996. ISBN 015201389X

Activity 65
Interactive Editing
Persuasive Writing

Goal
Students will read and write propaganda and advertising text with a critical eye.

Areas of Study
Language Arts, Social Studies, Mathematics, Science

Resources
Shared readings of information about a current topic of study
Enlarged brochures about the same topic of study
Posterboard, markers, correction tape

Lessons

- As a class, read the shared reading about a current topic of study.

- Discuss the text structure, as well as the type of information conveyed.

- As a class, read the enlarged brochures. Again discuss the text structure and the information conveyed.

- Engage the students in a discussion about the effect each type of text had on them as readers. Suggest that readers should always ask themselves the purpose for a text, as well as the format chosen.

- As a class, create a brochure advertising a topic related to the current area of study, using a second shared reading about a town, a product, or a school.

- Together, read the second shared reading. Engage the students in discussions about how the text should be revised.

Extensions

- Negotiate and interactively write strategies for reading advertisements with a critical eye.

- In pairs or small groups, create brochures and pamphlets about future topics of study.

After analyzing several sample brochures, this class organized and worked together to create a brochure for their city.

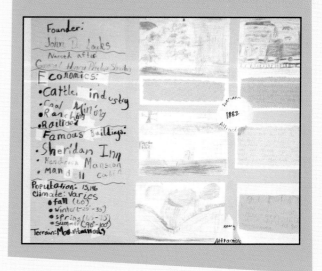

Additional Resources

Canfield, J. *Chicken Soup for the Kid's Soul: Stories of Courage, Hope, and Laughter.* Health Communications, Inc., 1998. ISBN 1558746099

Hesse, K. *Out of the Dust.* Scholastic, Inc., 1998. ISBN 0590371258

Hopkins, L.B. *Hand in Hand: An American History Through Poetry.* Simon & Schuster Children's, 1994. ISBN 067173315X

Activity 66
Interactive Editing
Resource Text Structures

Goal
Students will understand the organization and structure of resources in order to use them strategically and purposefully.

Area of Study
Language Arts

Resources
Shared reading from any content area
Shared reading of a dictionary entry
Magna Doodle, markers, poster paper, correction tape

Lessons
- With the class, read a shared reading relating to the current topic of study.

- As a class, choose a vocabulary word from the text that is difficult to understand.

- Discuss predictions for the word's meaning, emphasizing strategies the students are using to arrive at meaning.

- Confirm the predicted meanings, using a dictionary.

- Using an overhead or enlarged dictionary entry, with a different word, discuss specific conventions that are used.

- As a class, negotiate and interactively write a definition for the vocabulary word discussed above. Follow the conventions and formats of the actual dictionary entry modeled.

- Provide ample opportunities to discuss purposes for the conventions and formats, as well as other situations that would employ these same conventions and formats, such as parentheses, multiple word meanings, using words in examples, italics, and syllabication.

- Display the finished product for continued use as a model and resource for future reference.

Extensions
- Follow the steps outlined above for a thesaurus entry, encyclopedia, or any other resource. Provide opportunities to discuss the purposes and application of each. Also contrast the features of each, emphasizing how to decide when to use each specifically and purposefully.

- Using the dictionary entry written earlier, change it to a thesaurus entry or encyclopedia entry.

Additional Resources
Degross, M. *Donavon's Word Jar.* HarperTrade, 1999. ISBN 0060201916

Viorst, J. *The Alphabet From Z to A.* Simon & Schuster Children's, 1997. ISBN 068981545X

Wilbur, R. *The Pig in the Spigot.* Harcourt, 2000. ISBN 0152020195

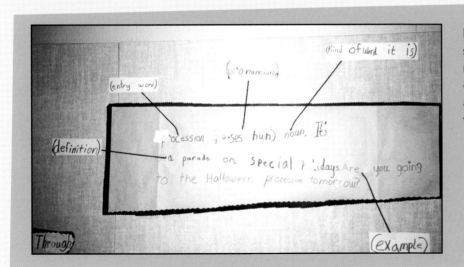

Following this activity, the students began using resources more readily and efficiently. They were also able to specifically identify their reasons for using them.

Activity 67
Interactive Editing
Scientific Method

Goal
Students will organize and record data, using the Scientific Method format.

Area of Study
Science

Resources
Shared reading of the Scientific Method
Shared reading of experiment procedure
Magna Doodle, markers, poster paper, correction tape

Lessons
- As a class, read and discuss the Scientific Method format as a shared reading.

- Discuss the possible purposes for this format.

- Read the shared reading experiment, discussing materials needed and procedures to follow.

- Conduct the class experiment, while the teacher or a student records informal notes and data gathered.

- Display an enlarged copy of the notes taken. Discuss the format and the information it conveys.

- Using the notes, interactively negotiate and rewrite the experiment into the Scientific Method format, referring to the shared reading as necessary.

- Engage the students in discussions regarding the importance of deciding which details to include and how to thoughtfully sequence information.

- Display the experiment for future reference.

Extensions
- In pairs or small groups, conduct more experiments requiring the students to use and organize information into the Scientific Method format.

- Provide sample, imaginary or authentic, notes recorded in a scientific journal related to the current topic of study. Have the students use and organize the information into the Scientific Method format.

Additional Resource
Kneidel, S. *Creepy Crawlies and the Scientific Method*. Fulcrum Publishing, 1993. ISBN 1555911188

Students used the information gathered in an experiment for making butter to complete and record the results of an investigation using the Scientific Method.

Activity 68
Interactive Editing
Study Skills

Goal
Students will understand expository text structure and identify important ideas.

Area of Study
Language Arts

Resources
Expository shared reading taken from current unit of study
Highlighter tape
Sentence Strips, Magna Doodle, correction tape

Lessons
- Read a shared reading relating to the current unit of study.

- Discuss any questions that come up as the students read, using the shared reading text as a source for answering questions.

- Emphasize that readers always need to ask themselves what the author is trying to say. This is comprehension.

- Explain that we're going to send a telegram to someone who knows nothing about the subject just read. Each word will cost $1.

- Tell them to reread the text and think about important words that could not be left out, but also keep in mind how expensive the telegram will be if too many words are included. As a guideline, choose one or two words per sentence. Highlight and discuss those words signalling importance in expository text.

- Highlight the key words for later reference.

- Divide the students into small groups and have them write a summary of the shared reading, using the least amount of key words possible.

- As a class, share and compare the different summaries.

Extensions
- As a class, arrange the key words into parts of speech. Have the students write topic sentences, supporting details, and summarizing sentences, using these key words. Arrange the sentences into paragraphs. In pairs or small groups, edit the sentences and paragraph organization.

- Using highlighted key words, write one-word summaries or phrases for each paragraph and organize them into an outline.

- Create outlines from independent reading of copies of informational text, using highlighters to identify important key words. Follow the process used above.

Additional Resources
Bampton, C., and Hawcock, D. *The Solar System*. Reader's Digest Children's Publishing, Inc., 1999. ISBN 1575842831

Berger, M. *Do Stars Have Points?: Questions and Answers About Stars and Planets*. Scholastic, Inc., 1999. ISBN 0590130803

Steele, P. *Black Holes and Other Space Phenomena*. Larousse Kingfisher Chambers, Inc., 1995. ISBN 1856975738

This class is identifying key words in order to study the solar system. This same activity is repeated, using a detailed shared reading, for every unit of study. Student engagement, understanding, and recall of information have increased with the adoption of these procedures.

Activity 69
Interactive Editing
Test Formats

Goal

Students will identify structures of test questions and develop strategies for determining appropriate responses.

Areas of Study

Language Arts, Social Studies, Mathematics, Science

Resources

Shared readings from any content area
Shared reading sample test questions for content area
 shared reading
Magna Doodle, markers, poster paper, correction tape

Lessons

- This activity should take place after the students have been immersed in a topic of study and are familiar with the subject matter.

- As a class, read and discuss a shared reading that represents essential content for the unit of study.

- Discuss ways a reader knows if he/she understands the ideas and concepts of what is read. Include the purposes for monitoring comprehension.

- Read and discuss the shared reading of sample multiple-choice test questions.

- Identify the types of questions they represent, and the kind of meaning they elicit, as well as the conventions and structures of the questions themselves.

- After the discussion, decide which answers would be correct. Emphasize the strategies used to decide on the correct answers.

- Think aloud the strategies used when constructing test questions.

- As a class, negotiate a question related to the shared reading, as well as options for multiple-choice answers. Allow the students to be part of the decision-making and construction of the format for the test questions.

- Display the test questions for future reference.

Extensions

- Rewrite the multiple-choice test question into a short-answer response. Discuss what the question is asking, along with the strategies used to arrive at an appropriate response. Interactively write a sample answer for future reference.

- Rewrite the test questions into extended responses, following the same procedure outlined for short-answer response questions.

- Interactively construct and write strategies for test-taking situations.

- In pairs or individually, write additional test questions for the current topic of study. Compile these for an end-of-unit quiz bowl.

Additional Resources

O'Malley, K. *Testing Miss Malarky*. Walker Publishing Company, Inc., 2000. ISBN 0802787371

Seuss, D. *Hooray For Diffendoofer Day!* Random House, Inc., 1998. ISBN 0679890084

After just one test-writing activity similar to the one described above, the students became significantly more aware of purposes and structures for test questions. They were able to describe possible strategies the test author may have used when choosing and arranging multiple-choice options.

Activity 70
Interactive Editing
Writing Process

Goal
Students will understand and purposefully use the writing process during independent writing.

Area of Study
Language Arts

Resources
Pictures of students writing independently
Magna Doodle, markers, poster paper, correction tape

Lessons
- During whole-group interactive writing, direct the students' attention to the writing process being modeled and followed.
- Provide direct, explicit instruction, labeling the steps followed throughout the interactive writing activities.
- Encourage the students to use the same procedures and strategies when writing independently.
- Provide ample time for practice in independent writing, giving feedback as necessary.
- When the writing process is familiar to most of the students, discuss ways to explain it in writing.
- Provide examples of instructions for other "how-to" activities.

- As a class, decide upon how text should be worded and arranged.
- Again, explicitly state that this interactive writing will be used as a reference and reminder of steps to be followed when engaged in any writing.

Extensions
- Discuss varieties of text formats and genres used by the class. Using the Writer's Workshop instructions as a template, negotiate and interactively write instructions for specific genres and text styles.
- After completing an experiment or specific activity, as a class negotiate and write the steps needed to repeat the event, referring to the Writer's Workshop model as necessary.

Additional Resources
Fletcher, R. *LIVE Writing: Breathing Life Into Your Words.* Avon Books, Inc., 1999. ISBN 0380797011

Fletcher, R. *How Writers Work: Finding A Process That Works For You.* HarperCollins Publishers, 2000. ISBN 038079702X

Myers, T. *Basho and the Fox.* Marshall Cavendish Inc., 2000. ISBN 0761450688

These are writing process steps negotiated and interactively written by students. The pictures were taken following the writing, after much discussion about what the pictures should represent.

Activity 71
Interactive Editing
Business Writing

Goal
Students will organize and write an informational memo.

Areas of Study
Language Arts, Social Studies, Mathematics, Science

Resources
Shared reading
Magna Doodle, markers, poster paper, correction tape

Lessons
- Read a shared reading relating to the current topic of study.

- Explain that this information needs to be included in a message to a specific audience. This audience may include a principal, business, teacher, or parent.

- Discuss the difference between personal and impersonal language. Discuss specific situations requiring the use of each, as well as specific audiences.

- As a class, summarize and negotiate text while the teacher provides guidance for the proper construction of memos.

- Highlight key words in the memo in order to interactively write an informational memo.

Extensions
- Individually or in pairs, write memos exploring other formats, such as formal or informal.

- Take the message from a formal memo and write an informal postcard.

- Divide the students into groups or pairs. Give each group or pair a different article or page from an article about the current topic of study. After reading the text, each group or pair writes a memo to the class covering the information in the article. Edit for spelling, punctuation, and meaning before distributing the memos to the class. Each student compiles a book of memos for unit information and references for memo styles and formats.

Additional Resources
Hobbie, H. *Toot and Puddle.* Little, Brown & Company, 1997. ISBN 0316365521

Leedy, L. *Postcards From Pluto.* Holiday House, Inc., 1997. ISBN 0823412377

Moss, M. *Luv, Amelia, Luv Nadia.* Pleasant Company Publications, 1999. ISBN 1562478230

To: Mr. Finley
From: Mrs. Weston's Class

As you know, our Class has been invited to attend the Science Fair at Crescent Elk Middle School. We will leave at 10:00.
We will be going with Mrs. Benson's class.

The class wrote an informational memo to the principal about their upcoming trip to the science fair.

Activity 72
Interactive Editing
Writing Process

Goal

Students will learn how to develop paragraphs, using a variety of text types as models.

Areas of Study

Language Arts, Social Studies, Mathematics, Science

Resources

Two texts in one series or two book chapters using the same text type.

Lessons

- Complete an interactive writing of one paragraph based on a book that is part of a series . Choose an example about one animal, such as an elephant.

- Select a second book in that series, such as one about lions.

- Identify the key vocabulary words in the new text or text chapter.

- Instead of writing a paragraph by paraphrasing using the key vocabulary, substitute those words into the text written about elephants.

- Continue the interactive editing of the new paragraph, making necessary substitutions to change the topic from elephants to lions.

- Compare the new paragraph with the model from the first paragraph.

- Discuss the form and style of informational writing.

Extensions

- Make a list of the steps in writing a paragraph using word substitution.

- Describe and discuss the characteristics of informational writing. Emphasize going from details to the main idea in a bottom up writing process.

Additional Resources

Chinery, M. *The Kingfisher Illustrated Encyclopedia of Animals*. Larousse Kingfisher Chambers, Inc., 1992. ISBN 185697801X

Meadows, G., Vial, C. *Dominie World of Animals: Lions*. Dominie Press, 2000. ISBN 0768509211

Meadows, G., Vial, C. *Dominie World of Animals: Elephants*. Dominie Press, 2000. ISBN 076850516X

Pratt, K. *A Swim Through the Sea*. Dawn Publications, 1994. ISBN 1883220033

World Book. *Amazing Animals*. World Book, Inc., 1998. ISBN 0716645017

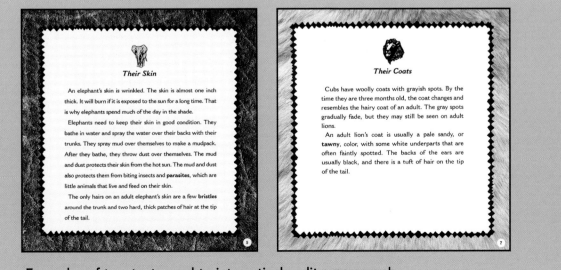

Their Skin

An elephant's skin is wrinkled. The skin is almost one inch thick. It will burn if it is exposed to the sun for a long time. That is why elephants spend much of the day in the shade.

Elephants need to keep their skin in good condition. They bathe in water and spray the water over their backs with their trunks. They spray mud over themselves to make a mudpack. After they bathe, they throw dust over themselves. The mud and dust protects their skin from the hot sun. The mud and dust also protects them from biting insects and **parasites**, which are little animals that live and feed on their skin.

The only hairs on an adult elephant's skin are a few **bristles** around the trunk and two hard, thick patches of hair at the tip of the tail.

Their Coats

Cubs have woolly coats with grayish spots. By the time they are three months old, the coat changes and resembles the hairy coat of an adult. The gray spots gradually fade, but they may still be seen on adult lions.

An adult lion's coat is usually a pale sandy, or **tawny**, color, with some white underparts that are often faintly spotted. The backs of the ears are usually black, and there is a tuft of hair on the tip of the tail.

Examples of two texts used to interactively edit a paragraph.

Activity 73
Interactive Editing
Using Word Walls

Goal
Students will begin to spell and analyze words they are using in their writing.

Areas of Study
Language Arts, Social Studies, Mathematics, Science

Resources
Word wall area in the classroom
Marker

Lessons
- Word walls support all content areas; in any text, key words carry the content of the subject field. Identifying and analyzing these words supports the learning of the content.

- During each unit of study, make a plan for identifying the key vocabulary.

- While reading the text, select the words that are central to the subject and write them on large sheets of paper with a dark marker. Stop as each word is encountered and record it in large print on the paper.

- Post the words on a wall in an area of the classroom that is easy to see. Alternatively, list the words on butcher paper.

- Label the wall by topic or book chapter.

- Sort the words in a specific way for analysis. For example, alphabetical, syllable length, or related root words.

- Keep the words as a resource on a chart or in a folder when the unit is finished.

Extensions
- Have a word wall or list for each chapter in the subject matter textbook. Use the words for spelling practice, word analysis, or for the study of parts of speech, root words, or suffixes.

- Make a classroom dictionary for each subject field, using the identified word wall terms. Make the dictionary cumulative for the semester or year.

Additional Resources
Frasier, D. *Miss Alaineus (A Vocabulary Disaster)*. Harcourt Inc., 2000. ISBN 0152021639

Levitt, P. *The Weighty Word Book*. Rinehart Publishers, 1999. ISBN 1570983135

Wilbur, R. *The Disappearing Alphabet*. Harcourt Inc., 1998. ISBN 0152014705

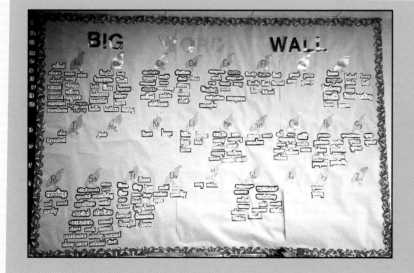

The word wall shown here was built over time to develop key vocabulary for students to use as a resource.

Activity 74
Interactive Editing
Paragraph Development

Goal
Students will develop paragraphs by identifying key vocabulary, paraphrasing, and summarizing original text.

Areas of Study
Language Arts, Science

Resources
Science text chapter or lab lesson
Butcher paper
Transparency of text selection
Marker, colored paper

Lessons
- Do a routine interactive editing of an error-free text selection.

- Identify key vocabulary, do paraphrasing, and write a summary sentence.

- Turn the paraphrase and summary sentence into a four-sentence paragraph. The summary sentence is the first sentence in the paragraph. Each sentence is paraphrased. The sentences are used to develop a new paragraph.

- Put each sentence on butcher paper strips and back them with colored paper. Put the summary/opening sentence on one color. Then put the paraphrased sentences on another color.

- Write a concluding sentence by rearranging the summary sentence. Flip or restate the subject and predicate sections of the summary sentence to make a concluding sentence.

- Put the concluding sentence on a third color of backing paper.

- Label each section of the paragraph with the terms: main idea, details, and concluding sentence.

- Post the paragraph on a classroom wall as an artifact to help remind the students of the form of a paragraph for future writing.

Extension
- Interactively write a definition of a paragraph and put it above the example.

Additional Resources
Auzou, P. *Big Book of Knowledge: Over 1,250 Questions on Nature, History, Science, Technology, and Culture.* Barnes & Noble Books, 1997. ISBN 0760707065

Caney, S. *Steven Caney's Invention Book.* Workman Publishing Company, 1980. ISBN 0894800760

Yenne, B. *100 Natural Wonders of the World.* Bluewood Books, 1995. ISBN 0912517158

This paragraph model was written in a third grade classroom.

Activity 75
Interactive Editing
Following Procedures

Goal

Students will paraphrase difficult text, yet follow a specific format, in order to understand meaning.

Areas of Study

Language Arts, Social Studies, Mathematics, Science

Resources

Shared reading of *Robert's Rules of Order*
Magna Doodle, markers, poster paper, correction tape

Lessons

- Share with the class that in order to build a community where each individual is respected, they will be holding formal class meetings on a regular basis.

- Explain that there are situations where explicit procedures are followed.

- As a class, read *Robert's Rules of Order*.

- Discuss its purpose, emphasizing that it is a procedure to ensure respect and order for everyone.

- Explain that this is the format used by adults in many situations and official meetings.

- Provide opportunity for discussion regarding the meaning of the text. Discuss the format and the wording, emphasizing the difficulty with reading this type of text. Discuss possible strategies to be used in understanding meaning and procedures.

- As a class, paraphrase and negotiate text that will help them to understand and follow this format.

- Using interactive writing, complete a paraphrased version, following the same format as the shared reading.

Extensions

- Identify other situations in which *Robert's Rules of Order* could be used and apply this procedure to those situations. For example, student council or club meetings.

- Identify other situations that may require uniform procedures. As a class, negotiate and write procedures.

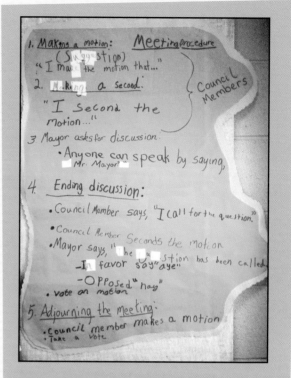

This paraphrased version of *Robert's Rules of Order* helped students to hold orderly and productive class meetings.

Additional Resources

Sheindlin, J. *Judge Judy Sheindlin's You Can't Judge a Book by Its Cover: Cool Rules for School.* HarperCollins Publishers, Inc., 2001. ISBN 0060294833

Sherman, J. *The New Robert's Rules of Order.* Barnes & Noble Books, 1999. ISBN 0760716463

Activity 76
Interactive Editing
Map Skills

Goal
The students will identify and define key words used for labeling world maps.

Area of Study
Social Studies

Resources
Social Studies text
Atlas
Classroom maps
Magna Doodle, chart paper, makers, correction tape

Lessons
- Study world maps from various sources.

- Make a list of common key terms used to label the various maps.

- Assign groups or pairs of students to research and define terms.

- Make a chart of the definitions.

- As a group, draw a world map for the class.

- Have the students label the map, using the definitions they wrote.

- Share read the finished product and leave it as a reference in the classroom.

Extensions
- In pairs or small groups, create other maps such as maps of the school, the neighborhood, and the city.

- Label these maps with appropriate words.

- Compare types of maps and labels and discuss the differences.

Additional Resources
Krull, K. *Wish You Were Here (Emily's Guide to the 50 States)*. Bantam Doubleday Dell Publishing Group, 1997. ISBN 038531146X

Lye, K., and Campbell, A. *Atlas in the Round*. Ivy Press Ltd., 1999. ISBN 0762406577

Petty, K., and Maizels, J. *The Amazing Pop-Up Geography Book*. Penguin Putnam Books for Young Readers, 2000. ISBN 0525464387

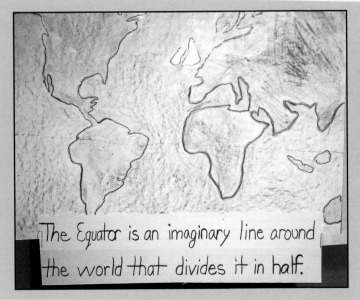

This class is beginning to label key definitions for maps.

Activity 77
Interactive Editing
Compare and Contrast

Goal
Students will recognize and use language to compare and contrast characters in narrative text.

Area of Study
Language Arts

Resources
Core literature story or novel, or basal text story
Magna Doodle, butcher paper, markers, correction tape

Lessons
- Divide the students into pairs. Have them answer five or six questions about themselves. How tall are they? What color is their hair? What color are their eyes? What are their favorite foods? What sports do they like? What are their favorite musical groups?

- Have the students write their answers on notebook paper.

- Have the students edit their answers for spelling.

- Draw a Venn diagram on the board.

- Use two student answers to model comparison and contrasts on a Venn diagram.

- Have students make an individual Venn diagram with their partner on notebook paper.

- Model a summary sentence. An example might be, "We have more similarities than differences."

- Share read a passage that describes a character in a story. Pick out key descriptive words.

- Have the students make a Venn diagram to compare and contrast themselves with the character in the story.

Extensions
- Share read an additional passage describing another character, highlighting key descriptive words.

- Have the students create a Venn diagram comparing and contrasting a character from two different stories.

Additional Resources
Brett, J. *Hedgie's Surprise*. Penguin Putnam Books for Young Readers, 2000. ISBN 0399234772

Polacco, P. *Thank-you Mr. Falkner*. Penguin Putnam Books for Young Readers, 1998. ISBN 0399231668

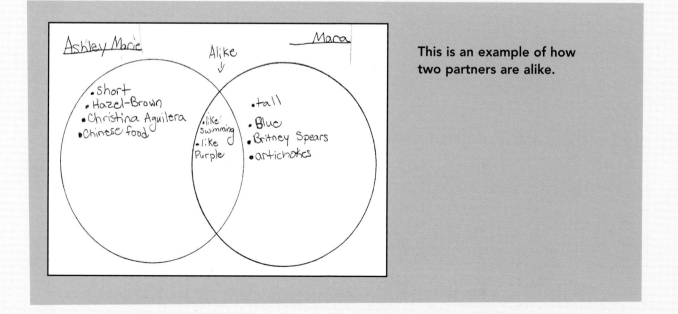

This is an example of how two partners are alike.

Activity 78
Interactive Editing
Compare and Contrast

Goal

The students will compare and contrast categories in mathematical language.

Area of Study

Mathematics

Resources

Shared reading of a question to investigate
Magna Doodle, chart paper, markers, correction tape

Lessons

- Share read a question to investigate. For example, write down and read the following questions: How many students have sisters? How many have brothers? How many have both? How many have neither?

- On chart paper have the students make a Venn diagram to display the results.

- Model language to produce a summary statement.

- As a class, negotiate and write a summary statement. For example, "More students in our class have both sisters and brothers than have just a sister or a brother," or "50 percent of the students in our class have both sisters and brothers."

- Display the completed Venn diagrams in the class as a reference.

Extensions

- In pairs or small groups, think of other questions to investigate.

- Research the questions with the class and make a Venn diagram to record the results.

- Create a book containing this information about the class. Use the book for independent reading.

Additional Resources

Manna, G. *You and Me*. Barefoot Books, 2000. ISBN 1841482633

Nolan, H. *How Much, How Many, How Far, How Heavy, How Long, How Tall is 1000?* Kids Can Press, Ltd., 1995. ISBN 1550741640

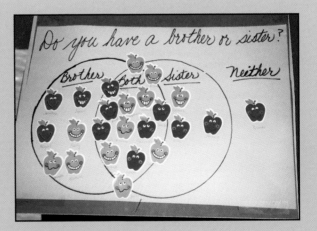

This class constructed a Venn diagram and interactively wrote the summary statement to compare and contrast information.

Activity 79
Interactive Editing
Reciprocal Teaching

Goal
The students will understand the role of the "student teacher" when using reciprocal teaching strategies by rewriting directions in their own words.

Areas of Study
Language Arts, Social Studies, Mathematics, Science

Resources
Overhead transparency of written directions for reciprocal teaching and individual student copies
Magna Doodle, chart paper, markers, correction tape

Lessons
- Share read directions for reciprocal teaching.
- Highlight key words that describe the role of the student teacher for prediction.
- Make a list of the key words.
- Rewrite the paraphrase on a bookmark that can be copied and laminated for students to refer to when acting as the teacher during reciprocal teaching.
- Negotiate and write directions for the student teacher for prediction.
- Post rewritten directions.

Extension
- Repeat using other reciprocal teaching terms.

Additional Resource
Choron, S., and Choron, H. *The Book of Lists for Kids.*
Houghton Mifflin Publishers, 1995. ISBN 039570815X

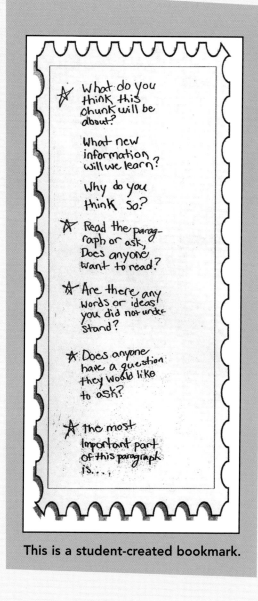

This is a student-created bookmark.

Directions for Reciprocal Teaching

Form small discussion groups of four to six students. Select one student to be the teacher. The "student teacher" facilitates the group discussion of a text selection, using the following steps:

1. **Predict.** Help the group make a guess about what the paragraph will say.
2. **Read.** Read aloud the selection.
3. **Clarify.** Ask whether there are any words or ideas that are unclear.
4. **Question.** Ask questions about important information in the selection.
5. **Summarize.** Paraphrase in one or two sentences what the selection was about.

Appoint a new student teacher and repeat the process.

Activity 80
Interactive Editing
Alternative Vocabulary Choices

Goal
The students will explore a variety of words to expand their vocabulary and make their writing interesting and varied.

Areas of Study
Language Arts, Social Studies, Mathematics, Science

Resources
Enlarged shared reading piece written by the teacher with an exaggerated use of the word *said*
Thesaurus, dictionary
Magna Doodle, markers, correction tape, chart paper

Lessons
- Share read the teacher's sample writing piece. Highlight *said* on the shared reading piece.

- Discuss the students' reaction to the use of the word *said*.

- Use reference materials and make a list of alternative words for the word *said*.

- As a class, rewrite the teacher's shared reading piece substituting new words for *said*.

- Share read the revised piece and display the list in the class for future reference.

Extensions
- Select a piece of literature or their own writing.

- Highlight *said* in the entire piece.

- Rewrite the piece, inserting new words for *said*.

Additional Resource
Henkes, K. *Chrysanthemum*. Morrow/Avon Books, 1996.
ISBN 0688147321

Ways to say "Said":

asked	screeched
answered	cried
replied	screamed
gasped	hollered
mumble	retorted
bellowed	ordered
demanded	squeaked
shouted	scolded
warned	roared
vowed	promised
	sneered

This class decided that *said* is dead.

Activity 81
Interactive Editing
Add One Adjective

Goal
Students will recognize and use descriptive words in their independent writing.

Areas of Study
Language Arts, Social Studies, Mathematics, Science

Resources
Enlarged text for shared reading of a selection using very simple, direct vocabulary and language structure
Dictionary, thesaurus
Magna Doodle, chart paper, markers, correction tape

Lessons
- Share read teacher written text containing simple, direct vocabulary and language structure.

- Have the students add one adjective like the word *little* as many places as they can in the text.

- Discuss the new piece and compare the two samples of writing.

- Use a dictionary, thesaurus, and samples from literature to make a list of describing words that could replace *little*.

- As a class, rewrite the shared reading piece, using new descriptive words, every time the word *little* appears.

- Share read the new passage and display it in the classroom for reference.

Extension
- Photocopy narrative pages from literature the class is reading. Give a page to each pair of students. Have each pair insert the same descriptive word wherever it fits in the passage. Trade the pages among classmates and have the students insert a variety of descriptive words for the single word in the passage. Collect the pages in a class book as samples of descriptive language.

Additional Resource
Heller, R. *Many Luscious Lollipops - A Book About Adjectives*. Putman, 1989. ISBN 0448031515

Sam's Cap   Dominie Press, Inc., 1998

Sam was a little black cat.
Sam had a little black cap.
Sam ran all around the backyard with his black cap.
Sam took a nap in the backyard.
Sam's cap blew away!
Sam ran after the cap.
Sam ran fast.
The cap went faster.
A man tried to catch the cap.
The man grabbed the cap with his hand.
Sam ran up to the little man.
The man put the cap back on Sam.
Sam was a happy cat.

Sam was a little black cat.
Sam had a little black cap.
Sam ran all around the *little* backyard with his *little* black cap.
Sam took a *little* nap in the *little* backyard.
Sam's *little* cap blew away!
Sam ran after the *little* cap.
Sam ran fast.
The *little* cap went faster.
A *little* man tried to catch the *little* cap.
The *little* man grabbed the *little* cap with his *little* hand.
Sam ran up to the *little* man.
The *little* man put the *little* cap back on Sam.
Sam was a happy *little* cat.

Students experimented with adding more descriptive language to text.

Activity 82
Interactive Editing
Setting Goals

Goal
Students will read, understand, and apply the language of a mission statement to their own writing.

Areas of Study
Language Arts, Social Studies

Resources
Shared reading copies of mission statements from a variety of organizations such as the school, the school district, or a local business

Magna Doodle, chart paper, markers, correction tape

Lessons
- Share read two mission statements. Discuss their purpose.

- Highlight and list key words from the two mission statement examples.

- Create a list of the words that are common to both lists.

- As a class, negotiate a text and write a classroom mission statement. Use as many of the key words as possible.

- Read, display, and refer to the class mission statement throughout the year.

Extensions
- Individually, or in pairs, discuss and write personal mission statements for the year.

- Discuss other school organizations that might need mission statements, like the student council, or the safety patrol.

- In small groups, write a mission statement for the organizations.

Additional Resources
Betz, A., *Treasury of Quotations for Children*. Scholastic, 1998. ISBN 0590271466

Katz, B. *We the People*. Greenwillow, 2000. ISBN 068816532X

A fifth grade class wrote this group mission statement.

It can be said that the best teacher is an informed teacher.

Assessment

Supporting children's learning is dependent on knowing what they know. For teaching to be both effective and efficient, it is important to know what skills each child has and what skills still need to be learned. Without this kind of specific information, instruction can only be general at best. Three instruments have been provided for teacher use in interactive writing and interactive editing.

Writing Checklist

The Writing Checklist is a simple system of notation that helps teachers keep track of item knowledge for each child. It is also a useful reminder to teachers about what skills they need to be thinking about in their teaching. The Writing Checklist is not a test. It is a way to monitor the writing skills each child can use. The form can be reproduced for each child.

Writing Rubric

The Writing Rubric can be used to track the overall writing level for individual students. The various levels and the accompanying performance indicators are for instructional rather than evaluation purposes.

Procedural Checklist and Self-Assessment

Two Procedural Checklists are provided, one for interactive writing and one for interactive editing. These checklists are designed to remind teachers what steps are needed to plan and implement a lesson. As a self-assessment, its only purpose is to inform your teaching.

9. Writing Checklist

The Writing Checklist is provided as a resource for teachers to record skill acquisition for each child. This checklist is not designed to be used as a test.

The source of this information is the teacher's observation of writing behaviors in classroom activities. There is no regular order in which children will exhibit these skills.

NOTE: This checklist may be duplicated for each child.

Alphabet
NOTE: Assess the children's ability to name and form letters prior to instruction so that you can tailor your teaching to each child's needs.

Recognizes and names letters. (Circle those the child knows.)

a b c d e f g h i j k l m n o p q r s t u v w x y z

A B C D E F G H I J K L M N O P Q R S T U V W X Y Z

Forms letters. (Circle those the child has mastered.)

a b c d e f g h i j k l m n o p q r s t u v w x y z

A B C D E F G H I J K L M N O P Q R S T U V W X Y Z

Phonemic Awareness (✓ when demonstrated)
__ Sings or recites the alphabet

__ Claps syllables in words

__ Counts syllables in multisyllabic words

__ Recognizes rhymes

__ Produces rhyme

__ Blends segmented sounds to say words

__ Blends different beginning sounds with phonograms (onset and rime)

__ Segments sounds in monosyllabic words

__ Manipulates sounds by substituting one sound for another

__ Manipulates sounds by adding or subtracting one sound for another

Phonics

Associates these basic sounds with the appropriate alphabet letter. (Circle those the child has mastered.)

/b/ b	/k/ c	/d/ d	/f/ f	/g/ g	/h/ h
/j/ j	/k/ k	/l/ l	/m/ m	/n/ n	/p/ p
/kw/ q	/r/ r	/s/ s	/t/ t	/v/ v	/w/ w
/ks/ x	/y/ y	/z/ z			

Associates these alternative sounds with the appropriate consonant letters.
(Circle those the child knows.)

/s/ c	/j/ g		
/ch/ ch	/sh/ sh	/th/ th	/hw/ wh

Writes words with these initial consonant blends.
(Circle those the child knows.)

br	cr	dr	fr	gr	pr	tr	wr
bl	cl	fl	gl	pl	sl		
sc	sk	sm	sn	sp	st	sw	
scr	squ	str	spr	spl	shr	sch	
dw	tw	thr					

Writes words with these final consonant blends.
(Circle those the child knows.)

ct	ft	lt	nt	pt	rt	st
ld	nd	rd	nk	sk	mp	nc(e)

(✓ When demonstrated)

__ Writes words with short ă, as in *cat*

__ Writes words with short ĕ, as in *bed*

__ Writes words with short ĭ, as in *trip*

__ Writes words with short ŏ, as in *box*

__ Writes words with short ŭ, as in *rug*

__ Writes consonant-vowel-consonant patterns

__ Writes consonant-vowel-consonant-consonant patterns

Writes words with long ā

 __ spelled a as in *paper*

 __ spelled a-consonant-e as in *game*

 __ spelled ai as in *rain*

 __ spelled ay as in *play*

Writes words with long ē

 __ spelled e as in *eat*

 __ spelled ee as in *feed*

 __ spelled e-consonant-e as in *these*

 __ spelled e as in *he*

 __ spelled eo as in *people*

Writes words with long ī

 __ spelled i-consonant-e as in *like*

 __ spelled ie as in *tried*

 __ spelled y as in *my*

 __ spelled i as in *Irene*

Writes words with long ō

 __ spelled o-consonant-e as in *home*

 __ spelled oa as in *road*

 __ spelled ow as in *mow*

 __ spelled oe as in *toe*

 __ spelled o as in *go*

 __ spelled oh

Writes words with long ū

 __ spelled u-consonant-e as in *tune*

 __ spelled ue as in *Tuesday*

 __ spelled u as in *music*

 __ spelled ugh as in *Hugh*

 __ spelled eau as in *beautiful*

 __ spelled oo as in *noon*

 __ spelled ou as in *youth*

 __ spelled o as in *who*

Writing Skills

Print Awareness (✓ when demonstrated)

__ Draws pictures and writes letter-like symbols to represent print

__ Writes letters to represent words related to a picture

__ Can write out where text begins (top left)

__ Writes a line of print from left to right

__ Moves from right-hand end of one line to left-hand beginning of next

__ Leaves spaces between words

__ Recognizes when sentences begin and end by using capital letters and appropriate punctuation

__ Demonstrates that a period indicates the end of a sentence (.)

__ Demonstrates that a question mark indicates a sentence asks a question (?)

__ Demonstrates that an exclamation mark indicates the sentence should be read with excitement or surprise (!)

__ Demonstrates the quotation marks come before and after words said by a character (" ")

__ Demonstrates correct usage of a comma (,)

__ Demonstrates correct usage of a colon (:)

__ Demonstrates correct usage of a semicolon (;)

Vocabulary

Writes high frequency words. (Circle those the child writes accurately.)

a	about	all	an	and	are
as	at	be	been	but	by
call	can	come	could	day	did
do	down	each	find	first	for
from	get	go	had	has	have
he	her	him	his	how	I
if	in	into	is	it	its
like	long	look	made	make	many
may	more	my	no	not	now
number	of	oil	on	one	or
other	out	part	people	said	see
she	so	some	than	that	the
their	them	then	there	these	they
this	time	to	two	up	use
was	water	way	we	were	what
when	which	who	will	with	word
would	write	you	your		

__ Understands and uses compound words appropriately

__ Understands and uses contractions appropriately

__ Word choice varies

Sentence Structure and Grammar

__ Uses subject-verb agreement

__ Uses modifiers

__ Adjectives

__ Adverbs

__ Uses prepositional phrases

__ Uses descriptive phrases

__ Uses simple sentences

__ Uses compound sentences

__ Uses complex sentences

__ Uses appropriate parts of speech

Writing Process

__ Is able to develop an idea

__ Organizes text

__ Understands procedures for outlining

__ Organizes prewriting by using various means of graphic organizers

__ Uses a variety of writing styles

__ Writes for a variety of purposes

__ Is able to develop a paragraph

During the Writing

How was each scribe chosen?

☐ Knew child could be successful   ☐ _____

☐ Used variety of children   ☐ _____

How was engagement sustained?
Which of the following were referred to? List examples and students involved:

☐ Word Wall _____

☐ Name Chart _____

☐ ABC Chart _____

☐ Interactive Writings _____

☐ Shared Readings _____

☐ Other Materials _____

Writing strategies used; list examples and students involved.

☐ "In Your Head" _____

☐ "In the Room" _____

☐ Stretch/Analogy _____

☐ Is there a part of the word that you know? _____

☐ Does it look right? _____

How was the text reread?

☐ After each new word   ☐ By phrase for fluency   ☐ At the completion

How were connections to previous learning made? (i.e., "Remember when we wrote about the flowers yesterday?")

_____

_____

List specific prompts used to help students transfer skills from interactive writing to their own independent work. (i.e., "When you are writing by yourself at your seat, you could use the word wall to help yourself, just like we did when we wrote the word _because_".)

After the Writing

What kind of artwork or illustrations accompanied the text?
Were the children involved in assembling the final product?
What are the plans for further use of this text?

Teaching Points Checklist

Which of the following teaching points were included during instruction?

Note: In any one lesson, a teacher may refer to only a few teaching points. Over time all teaching points will be addressed.

Alphabetic Principle
- Letter recognition
- Letter formation and handwriting
- Letter-name correspondence
- Letter-sound correspondence
- Alphabetic order

Concepts about Print
- Directionality
- One-to-one matching
- Return sweep
- Spacing, indentation, paragraph form, charts, text layout
- Concept of first and last part of word, sentence, story
- Punctuation, reading the punctuation

Phonemic Awareness and Phonics
- Hearing sounds in words
- Inflectional endings
- Rhyming
- Syllabication
- Compound words
- Onset and rime
- Segmentation
- Chunking and blending
- Root words
- Sounds in sequence
- Analogy
- High frequency words
- Spelling patterns
- Consonants, blends, short and long vowels, digraphs, diphthongs

Alliteration
- Suffixes, prefixes, root words
- Metaphors, similes

Written Language Conventions
- Punctuation and capitalization
- Spelling and word analysis
- Sentence structure

Grammar
- Proofreading and editing
- Parts of speech
- Word usage
- Irregular words
- Onomatopoeia
- Contractions

Writing Process
- Idea development
- Text organization
- Outlining and graphic organizers
- Vocabulary and word choice
- Concept development
- Categories of writing
- Paragraph development

12. Interactive Editing Procedural Checklist and Self-assessment

Planning for the lesson:

What observations and/or assessment informed instruction?

What standards were addressed?

What environmental print supported the work? Indicate how.

☐ Word Wall(s)   ☐ Informational Chart

☐ Interactive Writing   ☐ Shared Reading

☐ Interactive Editing

What writing category was used?

☐ Content Area Writing   ☐ Directions/How to   ☐ Definitions
☐ Graphic Organizers   ☐ Memo   - dictionary
☐ Key Word Banks   ☐ Editorial Article   - thesaurus
☐ Scientific Method   ☐ Telegram   - parts of speech
☐ Summary Statement   ☐ Telephone Message   ☐ Rules
☐ Test Questions   ☐ Steps of writing process

Before the Writing

What was considered when choosing the "error-free" text?

☐ Readability level

☐ Length of passage

☐ Prior knowledge of content

☐ Relevancy to grade level standards

What type of interactive editing best suits the purpose?

☐ Key Content Words   ☐ Paraphrase   ☐ Summary

How was the text read prior to the interactive editing lesson?

☐ Read aloud by the teacher

☐ Share read by teacher and students

☐ Reread by teacher and/or students

During the Writing

How was the learning scaffolded during the lesson?

☐ Lesson was done together as a class   ☐ Students worked with a class partner

☐ Students worked with others in their group or table   ☐ Teacher monitored all students working

☐ Modeled then provided support for student approximations

How was engagement sustained?
Which of the following were referred to? List examples.

☐ Word Wall   ☐ Informational Charts   ☐ Interactive Editings

_____   _____   _____

☐ Interactive Writing   ☐ Shared Readings   ☐ Other Materials

_____   _____   _____

_____   _____   _____

How were writing strategies modeled, discussed, and explicitly taught?

☐ Determine "idea chunk"   ☐ Discuss important words   ☐ Ask, "Does it make sense?"

_____   _____   _____

☐ Convey main idea   ☐ Ask, "Does it look right?"   ☐ Other

_____   _____   _____

How was the text reread?

☐ After each new sentence   ☐ Repeatedly for fluency   ☐ At the completion of the piece for comprehension

☐ _____   ☐ _____

How did you make connections to previous learning?

What specific prompts were used to help children transfer skills from interactive editing to their own independent work?

☐ _____

☐ _____

☐ _____

After the Writing

What kind of activities or extensions will connect to this experience?

How will the text be displayed or referred to during other portions of the day?

What are the plans for further use of this text?

Will anything be done differently next time? Why or why not?

Teaching Points Checklist

Which of the following teaching points were included during instruction?
Note: In any one lesson, a teacher may refer to only a few teaching points. Over time all teaching points will be addressed.

Phonemic Awareness

- Recognizes syllables
- Recognizes and produces rhymes
- Blending, substituting, manipulating sounds
- Onset and rime

Phonics

- Letter-sound correspondence
- Consonants
- Alternative consonant sounds
- Short vowels
- Long vowels
- Vowel combinations
- Initial blends
- Final blends

Written Language Skills

- Punctuation and capitalization
- Spelling and word analysis
- Grammar
- Parts of speech
- Word usage

Writing Process

- Idea development
- Text organization
- Outlining
- Vocabulary and word choice
- Concept development
- Categories of writing
- Paragraph development
- Proofreading and editing
- Paraphrasing
- Summarizing

Handwriting Model

a Go around to the left; then back up, and down.

 **A** Slant down to the left; slant down to the right; Make a line across.

b Go straight down; then back up, and around to the right.

B Make a straight line down. Go back to the top. Go around to the right and around to the right again.

c Go to the left and around; then stop.

 C Go to the left and around; then stop.

d Go to the left and around; then straight up and down.

 **D** Make a straight line down. Go back to the top and go around right to the bottom.

e Go straight to the right; then around and stop.

 **E** Make a straight line down. Then go right at the top, the middle, and the bottom.

Handwriting Model

f Go around left and straight down. Make a little line across.

F Make a straight line down. Then go right at the top and in the middle.

g Go left and around. Then go up and down and around to the left to make a hook.

G Go to the left and around; then turn and make a little straight line to the left.

h Go straight down, then back up, around to the right, and down.

H Make a straight line down. Make another one beside it. Then draw a straight line between the two.

i Go straight down and make a dot on top.

I Make a straight line down. Put little lines across the top and bottom.

j Go straight down and curve the bottom around to the left. Make a dot on top.

J Go straight down; then curve to the left at the bottom.

k   Make a line straight down. Make a slanted line to the left and then back to the right.

K   Make a line straight down. Make a slanted line left from the top to the middle; then go down and right.

i   Make a line straight down.

L   Go straight down; then straight to the right.

m   Make a line straight down; then go back up and over, and back up and over again.

M   Go straight down. Start back at the top; slant down, slant up, then go straight down.

n   Make a line straight down; then go back up and over one time.

N   Go straight down. Start back at the top; slant down and go straight back up.

o   Go all the way around to the left.

O   Go all the way around to the left.

Handwriting Model

p Go straight down; then back up and around to the right.

P Go straight down; then start back at the top and curve around right and back.

q Go around to the left; then up, then straight down and make a tail.

 Go all the way around to the left. Then make a little line at the bottom slanting right.

r Go straight down; then back up, over, and stop.

R Go straight down. Start back at the top; curve around right and back; then make a slanted line down and right.

s Go around one way; then switch and go around the other way.

S Go around one way; then switch and go around the other way.

 Make a line straight down; then make a little line across.

 Go straight down; then make a line straight across at the top.

 u   Go down, around, back up, and down.

 U   Go straight down; curve around right; go straight back up.

 v   Slant down to the right; then slant back up.

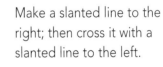 V   Slant down to the right; then slant back up.

 w   Slant down to the right; then slant back up; then go back down and up again.

 W   Slant down to the right, then slant back up, then go back down and up again.

x   Make a slanted line to the right; then cross it with a slanted line to the left.

 X   Make a slanted line to the right; then cross it with a slanted line to the left.

y   Make a slanted line to the right. Then make a longer slanted line to the left.

 Y   Slant halfway down and go back up. Then at the bottom make a straight line down.

z   Go straight right; slant left and down; go straight right again.

 Z   Go straight right; slant left and down; go straight right again.

Phonics Skill Charts

Words with *ai* Phonograms

ain	air	aid	ail	ait
gain	fair	laid	bail	bait
lain	hair	maid	fail	gait
main	lair	paid	Gail	wait
pain	pair	raid	hail	trait
rain	chair	braid	jail	strait
vain	flair	staid	mail	
brain	stair	afraid	nail	
chain			pail	
grain			quail	
plain			rail	
Spain			sail	
stain			tail	
train			wail	
sprain			frail	
train			snail	
			trail	

Words with the Phonogram *ay*

bay	ray	pray
day	say	spay
gay	way	stay
hay	bray	sway
jay	clay	tray
lay	flay	spray
may	fray	stray
nay	gray	away
pay	play	today

Words with *ea* Phonograms

ead	east	eat	ear	eal	ea	eak	eam
bead	beast	beat	dear	deal	lea	beak	beam
lead	feast	feat	fear	heal	pea	leak	ream
read	least	heat	gear	meal	sea	peak	seam
	yeast	meat	hear	peal	tea	teak	team
		neat	near	real		weak	cream
ean	**eap**	peat	rear	seal		bleak	dream
bean	heap	seat	tear	teal		creak	gleam
dean	leap	bleat	year	veal		sneak	scream
jeans	reap	cheat	clear	zeal		speak	steam
lean	cheap	cleat	shear	squeal		squeak	stream
mean		pleat	smear	steal		streak	
wean		treat	spear				
clean		wheat					

Phonics Skill Charts

More Words with *ee* Phonograms

eet	ee	eel	een	eed	eep	eek	eem
beet	bee	feel	seen	deed	deep	leek	deem
feet	fee	heel	teen	feed	jeep	meek	seem
meet	see	keel	green	heed	keep	peek	teem
fleet	tee	peel	sheen	need	peep	seek	
greet	wee	reel	queen	reed	seep	week	
sheet	flee	creel	screen	seed	weep	cheek	eer
sleet	free	kneel		weed	creep	creek	beer
street	glee	steel		bleed	cheep	Greek	deer
sweet	knee	wheel		breed	sleep	sleek	jeer
tweet	three			creed	steep		peer
	tree			freed	sweep		sneer
				greed			steer
				speed			
				steed			
				treed			

Words with oa Phonograms

oat	oast	oad	oach	oak	oal	oam	oan
boat	boast	load	coach	oak	coal	foam	loan
coat	coast	road	poach	soak	foal	loam	moan
goat	roast	toad	roach	cloak	goal	roam	groan
moat	toast			croak	shoal		
bloat							
float							
throat							

More Words with *oo* Phonograms

oon	oo	ool	oom	oot	ood	oop
boon	boo	cool	boom	boot	food	coop
moon	coo	fool	doom	coot	mood	goop
noon	goo	pool	loom	loot	brood	hoop
soon	moo	drool	room	moot		loop
croon	too	spool	zoom	root		droop
spoon	woo	stool	bloom	toot		scoop
swoon	zoo	school	broom	shoot		sloop
	shoo		gloom	snoot		snoop
			groom			swoop
						troop

More Words with *ow* Phonograms

ow	own
bow	own
low	sown
mow	blown
row	flown
sow	grown
tow	known
blow	shown
flow	
glow	
grow	
know	
show	
slow	
snow	
stow	

More Words with *oo* Phonograms

ook	ood
book	good
cook	hood
hook	wood
look	stood
took	
brook	
crook	
shook	

Phonics Skill Charts

More Words with *oi* Phonograms

oil	oin
boil	coin
coil	join
foil	loin
soil	groin
toil	
spoil	

More Words with *oy*

boy	loyal	annoy
coy	royal	destroy
joy	oyster	employ
soy		enjoy
toy		
cloy		
ploy		

More Words with *ou* Phonograms

ouse	out	ound	oud	ount
douse	bout	bound	loud	count
house	gout	found	cloud	fount
louse	lout	hound	proud	mount
mouse	pout	mound		fountain
blouse	rout	pound		mountain
grouse	tout	round		
	about	sound		
	grout	wound		
	shout	around		
	spout	ground		
	stout	astound		
	trout			
	sprout			

More Words with *ow* Phonograms

ow	own	ower	owel	owl
bow	down	bower	towel	cowl
cow	gown	cower	vowel	fowl
how	town	dower	trowel	howl
now	brown	power		jowl
row	clown	tower		owl
sow	crown	flower		growl
vow	drown	glower		prowl
wow	frown	shower		scowl
chow				
plow				
prow				
scow				

Words with *ar* Phonograms

ar	ark	ard	art	arm	arn	arp
bar	bark	card	cart	farm	barn	carp
car	dark	hard	dart	harm	darn	harp
far	hark	yard	mart	charm	yarn	tarp
jar	lark	guard	part			sharp
mar	mark	shard	tart			
tar	park		chart			
char	shark		smart			
scar	spark		start			
spar	stark					
star						

Phonics Skill Charts

Words with *ir* Phonograms

ir	irl	irt
fir	girl	dirt
sir	swirl	flirt
stir	twirl	shirt
	whirl	skirt
		squirt

Words with *er* Phonograms

erb	erd	erk	erm
herb	herd	jerk	germ
verb	nerd	perk	term

Words with *ur* Phonograms

ur	urt	urn	urse
cur	curt	burn	curse
fur	hurt	turn	nurse
blur	blurt	churn	purse
slur	spurt	spurn	
spur			

Words with *or* Phonograms

ork	ort	ord	orn	orch
cork	fort	cord	born	porch
fork	port	ford	corn	torch
pork	short	lord	horn	scorch
York	snort	chord	torn	
stork	sport	sword	worn	
			scorn	
			sworn	
			thorn	

Glossary

Air writing. Using the fingers of one hand to write a letter or word in large movements in the air.

Alliteration. Repetition of initial sounds in several words or in a phrase or longer stretch of text.

Alphabetic principle. The concept underlying writing systems that each phoneme/sound should have its own grapheme/letter.

Analogy. General similarity in word components or meaning.

Artifacts. Memorable examples from a lesson, usually in writing, that students can refer to and use in other work in the classroom.

Blending. Combining of sounds in two or more letters.

Breaking down. Examining or analyzing a word, phrase, or sentence in all of its components: letters, sounds, spelling pattern, sentence structure.

Building up. Combining sounds, letters, and spelling patterns to make words, phrases, or sentences.

Chunk. Usually referring to a group of sounds, including the syllable unit, prefix, suffix, onset, rhyme, and phonograms.

Concepts about print. Basic elements of reading, including book handling, directionality, reading the punctuation, recognizing letters and words, and matching sound to letter.

Conventions. Standard patterns used in writing, such as spelling conventions, punctuation, and grammar.

Correction tape. Any type of blank tape that can cover an error and be written on to make a correction.

Decode. To analyze spoken or written symbols of a language in order to understand their intended meaning.

Digraph. Two letters that represent one speech sound.

Diphthong. A single vowel sound made from two vowel sounds in a syllable.

Directionality. The ability to perceive and use spatial orientation accurately.

Early strategies. The earliest "in the head" understandings a child uses to begin processing in reading and writing; these include directionality, one-to-one matching, and locating known and unknown words.

Edit. To correct or adjust an existing text to make a better piece of writing or to change the type of writing, such as changing genres.

Encode. To change a message into written symbols.

Error-free text. A piece of writing that is correct prior to editing for changes; usually from a printed text of some type.

Expository writing. A traditional form of composition designed to explain or set forth a point.

Extension activities. Suggestions for extending a lesson in a connected way.

Familiar text. A previously read text at the instructional or independent level.

Fluency. The ability to read with phrasing and expression.

Frustration level. When text is too difficult to decode and comprehend; usually at the 89% level or below, based on readability formulas or leveling of texts, and a running record.

Genre. A category system for classifying text, usually by form or content.

High frequency words. Words that occur very often in spoken or written language; often mistakenly called sight words.

Highlighter tape. Transparent tape that is used to point out a word; similar to a highlighter pen in purpose.

Independent level. When a child is able to decode and comprehend text for independent work; usually at the 95% level or above, based on readability formulas or leveling of texts, and a running record.

Inflectional ending. A suffix that changes the form or function of a root word, stem or compound, but not its basic meaning.

Innovation. An interactive writing process of varying the recording of a text that has been read for the purposes of understanding the sound/symbol relationship and the structure of the written sentence, and to support decoding and spelling. This may include changing a word or character, or adding a page to an existing text.

Instructional level. When a child is able to decode and comprehend text for instructional work; usually at the 90-95% level, based on readability formulas or leveling of texts, and a running record.

Irregular word. A word that does not follow a regular linguistic pattern or rule for its spelling or pronunciation.

Key content words. Terms in the reading or text that carry the basic information, usually 15-18% of the words in an average content area passage.

Magna Doodle. A commercial product used to write examples to support the teaching of interactive writing; uses a blunt instrument and board with magnetic shavings to form letters; available in various sizes.

Modifier. A word, phrase, or clause that modifies, changes, or adds to the meaning of another word, phrase, or clause.

Name chart. A classroom chart of the students' first and sometimes last names used to support phonics and spelling instruction in constructing interactive writing messages; in upper grades this might take the form of a list of presidents or other names.

Negotiation. An interactive writing process of creating text based on student discussion for the purposes of understanding the sound/symbol relationship and the structure of the written sentence, and to support decoding and spelling.

One-to-one matching. The ability of a reader to match one word said to one word read; an early reading skill.

Onomatopoeia. When the sound made by pronouncing a word suggests its meaning.

Onset. Usually the consonants preceding the vowel of a syllable.

Paraphrase. Restating the meaning of something spoken or written.

Phonemic awareness. The awareness of the sounds (phonemes) that make up spoken words.

Phonics. A method of teaching reading and spelling that stresses the sound/symbol relationship.

Phonogram. In word recognition, a sequence including a vowel and one or more ending consonants.

Phonological awareness. The awareness of the constituent sounds of words in learning to read and spell.

Phonology. The study of speech sounds and their function in a language.

Pointer. An implement such as a ruler or stick with a decoration on the end, or a similar item used to help with pointing to and rereading texts.

Predicate. In grammar, the part of a sentence that expresses something about the subject; often called a verb phrase.

Prompt. Language used by the teacher to draw the student's attention to a particular aspect of the reading process.

Read aloud. Sharing a story aloud, developing vocabulary, modeling structure and fluency, and introducing content.

Readability. A predictive formula for determining the difficulty level of a text by a ratio, usually the sentence length and syllable count.

Reciprocal teaching. A teaching strategy whereby teacher and students share the responsibility for conducting a discussion.

Reciprocity of reading and writing. The concept that reading and writing are supportive processes, and each one is learned more effectively by relating one to the other.

Return sweep. When the eyes reach the end of a line of print and move to the beginning of the next line on the same page.

Rhyme. Usually identical or sometimes very similar recurring final sounds in words.

Rime. A vowel and any following consonants of a syllable.

Segmentation. Dividing a word into its constituent phonemes.

Shared reading. Choral reading of a passage, usually a big book, to help develop early reading strategies, increase fluency, and extend phonological awareness.

Stretching words. Articulating a word slowly and distinctly in order to hear the component (segmented) sounds.

Subject. In grammar, the main topic of a sentence to which the predicate refers.

Summary statement. A bringing together of the key information in a passage.

Syllabication. The division of words into syllables.

Synthesize. To draw ideas together into a form of a summary.

Think aloud. To model thinking behaviors to students by talking though a process as it is happening, such as a think aloud during reading a story to a class.

Transcription. An interactive writing process of exactly recording the text that has been read for the purposes of understanding the sound/symbol relationship and the structure of the written sentence, and to support decoding and spelling.

Venn diagram. Overlapping circles used two show similarities and differences in semantic mapping.

Wikki Stix. A commercially made product using wax-covered string that can be used to highlight letters, words, parts of speech, punctuation, etc.

Word analysis. A general label for analyzing words into their constituent parts, including recognition of sight words; becomes progressively more difficult in polysyllabic words.

Word families. A group of words sharing a common phonic element.

Word wall. The use of print on walls that includes various types organized for instruction such as high frequency words, word families or rhyming words, and content area words.

Wordness. A term that defines the concept of word in print and refers to the appropriate use of spaces in and around words.

Written language conventions. The accepted norms of writing in both structure and punctuation.

Index